Best
Recipes of
Michigan
Inns and
Restaurants

Compiled and edited by:
Margaret E. Guthrie

Editorial assistance:
Annie L.J. Saart

Other books in this series:
Best Recipes of Wisconsin Inns and Restaurants, 1986.
Best Recipes of Minnesota Inns and Restaurants, 1987.

For additional copies of this book, contact:

Amherst Press
A division of Palmer Publications, Inc.
P.O. Box 296
Amherst, Wisconsin 54406

Table of Contents

Preface

By now, on this our third book, we have become a team. There is my publisher, Chuck Spanbauer and his talented, competent staff who translate my scratchings into a handsome and readable book. There is my editorial assistant, Annie Saart, who is becoming a mainstay. There is my attorney, Michael Davis, who resolves everything from contracts to speeding tickets and finally, my three children who are responsible for the maintenance of my sense of humor and who get to taste many of the test recipes.

For this book, the folk in Michigan who were particularly helpful and without whom it wouldn't be half the book it is: Jeremy Iggers of the Detroit Free Press; "Bud Taste" of Detroit Monthly Magazine; Dotti Clune of Western Michigan Magazine; Carolyn "Peachy" Rentenbach; Phil and Marjorie Dorman, old friends who opened their home to me in Detroit; Phyllis Farrell, of The Ample Pantry, a new friend whose help in Kalamazoo was invaluable. And most important of all, the chefs, restaurant owners and managers who were cooperative and enthusiastic; in particular Pete and Nancy Racine, my first Michigan restaurateurs, of the Grand Mere Inn in Stevensville. Thank you all and bon appetit!

Introduction

One of the unexpected dividends of doing these books of recipes from inns and restaurants in the upper Midwest is the education I am acquiring. I discovered Michigan's wine industry in touring the state. It's something of which Michiganers can be justifiably proud. Of the 47 states that produce wine, Michigan ranks third or fourth.

I also discovered that the same area that's so good for grapes is equally good for apples. Michigan is this country's third largest apple producer, shipping 26 million bushels to market in 1985. Michigan grows peaches, too! And their climate is nothing like Georgia's.

I found wonderful ethnic foods—there are several Ethiopian recipes in this book, for example. And, in Michigan, I found hospitality of the sort that is supposed to exist only in another region of the country. People in the restaurant business in Michigan were friendly, enthusiastic about my project, and very hospitable.

Often you will hear people say that anyone who wants to run a restaurant or cook for a living must be crazy. That may or may not be so, depending, I suppose, on your definition of crazy. I do find that many of the people who own, manage and cook in restaurants are devoted to the serving of good food in a way that few of us, who cook for our own sustenance and the occasional entertainment of friends, are.

It is encouraging to see real growth in the restaurant business other than the fast food chain type. Some of the restaurants in this book also offer a take out menu and one even offers home delivery of dinner, if you call before 4 o'clock in the afternoon. There is innovation and adaptation in the restaurant business that makes it really exciting right now. Sometimes it seems that we are a country that consumes little else other than the ubiquitous fast food offered everywhere. Michigan's restaurants refute that and you will find many wonderful recipes in this book to illustrate the new interest in food and its preparation.

Michigan's chefs also know how to take full advantage of the local game and produce. One of the things I ask when approaching the restaurants is for recipes that involve local foods. The response from the Michigan chefs was almost overwhelming. You will find recipes for everything from wild leeks and morels to venison and smoked whitefish. There is even a recipe for muskrat served by a restaurant in Wyandotte. This recipe is, in fact, the owner's favorite way of preparing muskrat. You can't ask for a better recommendation than that.

Michigan chefs are up on all the latest, too. There is an appetizer cheesecake, a strawberry shortcake using chocolate "shortcake," tempting appetizers, interesting new salads and variations of classic soup recipes. There are recipes for almost any occasion, from the very grand to dining alone and being good to yourself.

Let me recommend that when you select a Michigan menu for a dinner party, that you also select a Michigan wine or wines to go along with the food for the whole, true flavor of Michigan.

This is Michigan's sesquicentennial and I can think of no more fitting way to pay tribute to the state and its people than with this compendium of recipes from the best, most imaginative chefs in the state.

Michigan is a beautiful state with much to offer in other respects as well as this enticing look at the foods available wherever you choose to travel. Bon Appetit! from Michigan's chefs.

* * * * * * * * * * *

Before you set out to produce some of these recipes there are some things you might consider. First, these chefs ask that you read each recipe you intend to create all the way through. Be sure you have all the ingredients on hand and do not substitute one ingredient for another. If a recipe calls for Dijon mustard, use it, not yellow salad mustard.

Also a word about ingredients. As in most cookbooks, flour means all purpose white flour. If another flour is called for it will be specified as in unbleached or whole wheat. Butter means butter—other kinds such as unsalted or whipped will be specified. The same is true of sugar. Unless otherwise specified it is white, granulated sugar. Most of the recipes call for heavy cream and the distinction here is important. Some of the large dairies are "ultrapasteurizing" their whipping cream, thus destroying the taste, but prolonging the shelf life. Therefore, recipes in this book call for heavy cream, which also should be in the dairy case at your supermarket or grocery store. It is the same thing as whipping cream. Sometimes it will say heavy (gourmet) cream. The word gourmet occasionally appears in parentheses. That's what you want. If you don't see it, ask for it.

Use the freshest ingredients. When a recipe calls for lemon juice or Parmesan cheese, use fresh. Squeeze the lemon, grate the cheese. There is no comparison when it comes to taste and to flavor. And now, good cooking and good eating!

Brunch

Brunch

Brunch is that meal that combines the best of breakfast and luncheon. The word brunch has come to have a leisurely connotation to it. It is a meal taken at ease, on the weekends.

With more women than ever before working, with life lived at an increasingly hectic pace, brunch has become an attractive and easier way to entertain. It is also one of the most popular restaurant meals; there are restaurants whose entire culinary reputation is based on their weekend brunches.

Michigan's chefs are aware of all these things and have responded with a wonderful array of dishes appropriate for a brunch party. Or brunch for two. The difficulty here is trying to decide which to serve first, there are so many tempting sounding dishes from which to choose.

California Chili

6 tablespoons oil
1 large onion, chopped
5-6 cloves garlic, minced
1 green pepper, chopped
2 pounds stew beef, cut into
   1" cubes
2 tablespoons flour
1 can (6 ounces) tomato paste
2 cans (22 ounces) chili beans
3 cups good beef stock
¾ cup ketchup
3-4 fresh jalapeno peppers,
   minced
2 cans (28 ounces) tomatoes
2 tablespoons chili powder

In a heavy bottomed saucepan, saute onion, garlic, green pepper and beef in oil until the meat is nicely browned.

Sprinkle flour over beef/onion mixture and stir in until flour is absorbed.

Add remaining ingredients and simmer together until meat is tender, approximately 2 hours. Yield: 6 servings.

From: **The Hearthstone**
3550 Glade (Corner House Motel)
Muskegon, Michigan

Layered Cheese Tortas
with Fresh Tomato Salsa

6 9" flour tortilla shells
¼ cup salad oil
¾ pound thinly sliced
   cheddar cheese
¾ pound thinly sliced
   Monterey Jack cheese
3 tablespoons finely diced
   ripe olives
3 tablespoons finely diced
   green onions
3 tablespoons finely diced
   pimento
1½ avocados, finely diced
1-3 tablespoons finely diced
   jalapeno peppers, to taste
1 cup tomato salsa

Preheat oven to 350 degrees. Rub tortilla shells with a thin coating of salad oil and place on baking sheet in a single layer. Bake for 5-7 minutes until golden brown. Let cool. Increase oven temperature to 400 degrees.

Cover each shell with slices of cheddar and Monterey Jack cheese so none of the tortilla shell is exposed. Sprinkle each shell with 1 teaspoon of the ripe olives, green onions and pimento. Top with diced avocado, dividing evenly and jalapenos, ¼ teaspoon or to taste. Then spread on 1½-2 tablespoons of salsa. Make sure all ingredients are spread evenly and consistently.

Then place 3 shells on top of one another (you should now have 3 stacks of 3 shells). Place them on baking sheet and bake for 5 minutes until the cheese layer is well melted.

Cut each 3 layer torta into 8 wedges and stack them to make 4 wedges. You should now have twelve 6-layer wedges. Serve hot with sour cream and additional salsa. Yield: 12 wedges.

From:

**The Bay Cafe
at Lumberton**
1050 West Western Avenue
Muskegon, Michigan

Chicken with Pasta

2 pounds chicken breast meat,
    cut into strips
⅔ cup finely chopped onion
2 teaspoons garlic, minced
⅓ cup butter or oil
2 teaspoons basil
2 teaspoons oregano
freshly cracked pepper
½ pound zucchini
18 cherry tomatoes
2 cups shredded Swiss cheese
1 pound fettucine

Saute the chicken, onion and garlic in the butter. Add the basil, oregano and pepper. Add sliced zucchini. Saute just until tender, 5-10 minutes. Add cherry tomatoes and saute just until tomatoes are heated through, approximately 2 minutes. Sprinkle mixture with freshly grated pepper.

Serve over cooked fettucine and sprinkle with the Swiss cheese. The mixture can be placed in the oven to keep warm. This recipe is a favorite, colorful and sure to be a hit with you and yours.

From: **The Ample Pantry**
5629 Stadium Drive
Kalamazoo, Michigan

Fettucine al Burro

7 ounces melted butter
½ teaspoon dried basil
2 cups freshly grated
    Parmesan & Romano cheeses
1 teaspoon garlic powder
½ teaspoon salt
½ teaspoon nutmeg
2 pounds fettucine
small bunch Italian parsley

Put all ingredients except noodles and parsley together in a large bowl.

Bring a large kettle of water to a rolling boil, add the fettucine. Boil for 10-12 minutes, stirring to keep noodles from sticking together. Drain, reserving a cup of the hot water.

Immediately add the noodles to the other ingredients in the bowl and stir to blend the sauce ingredients with the noodles. The reserved hot water may be added if the sauce is too thick. The sauce should not be as thick as tomato sauce. Use the fresh parsley to garnish.

From: **Argiero's**
Italian Restaurant
2300 Detroit Street
Ann Arbor, Michigan

Fettucine Carlo

2 cups boneless chicken
    breast meat, ½-⅜" long
5 cups half & half
12 tablespoons freshly grated
    Parmesan cheese
2 teaspoons freshly ground
    black pepper
12 egg yolks, beaten
2 pounds fettucine, preferably
    fresh, but good frozen will do
1 teaspoon salt

Saute the chicken in butter for about 5 minutes over medium high heat, seasoning to taste with salt and pepper.

In a heavy bottomed saucepan, bring the cream, cheese, pepper, and egg yolks to a boil, stirring continously. Cook the fettucine in boiling water for 5-6 minutes if fresh and according to package directions if frozen. Do not overcook, fettucine should be al dente, soft but firm.

Add the chicken nuggets to the creamy sauce, stir. Add the sauce to the drained fet-

tucine, toss lightly. Sprinkle with freshly grated Parmesan and serve immediately. Fresh peas and/or parsley may be added for color.

From:

Monte Bianco Restaurant
962 Dix Street
Lincoln Park, Michigan

Casserole of Frog Legs Provencale

1¼ pounds frog legs
2 ounces olive oil
1 medium onion
2½ cups sliced mushrooms
4 tomatoes, skinned, seeded, julienned
½ teaspoon garlic, minced
⅛ cup white wine
2 cups freshly grated Parmesan cheese
4 tablespoons chopped parsley

Preheat oven to 350 degrees. Lightly flour the frog legs, saute in a pan with olive oil. When nicely browned, put the pan in the oven and bake until the meat feels firm. Take the meat off the bones and discard the bones. The meat should come off bones easily. If it doesn't, cook a little longer.

Saute the onion for 2 minutes, then add the mushrooms and saute for 2 more minutes. Add tomatoes and garlic and saute for 2 more minutes. Add white wine and reduce by ⅔. Put mixture in four 1-cup casserole dishes or one 4-6 cup casserole. Cover with the Parmesan cheese. Put the casserole(s) on a cookie sheet and bake for 25 minutes. Sprinkle generously with chopped parsley. Serve with a good French bread. Yield: 4 servings.

From:

Chez Raphael
2700 Sheraton Drive
Novi, Michigan

Brandywine
Lobster-Broccoli Mornay

2 pounds cooked lobster meat
12 medium size broccoli
   (stem and flower), blanched
12 large mushroom caps
4 cups Brandywine
   mornay sauce

Mornay Sauce:
¼ cup butter
¼ cup flour
3 cups half & half
¼ cup cheddar cheese
¼ cup Swiss cheese
2 tablespoons sherry

Seasoned Bread Crumbs:
2 cups soft bread crumbs
salt to taste
¼ cup grated Parmesan cheese
   (more if needed)
1 tablespoon melted butter

For the mornay sauce, put butter and flour in a heavy bottom saucepan over medium heat. Stir, cooking until flour and butter are well blended. Add the preheated half & half, stirring constantly, until smooth and thickened. Add the cheeses and sherry and stir until the cheese has melted.

Preheat oven to 400 degrees. Arrange 5 ounces of the lobster meat in each of 6 individual casserole dishes (can be combined in one large casserole dish, if desired). Place one spear of broccoli on each side of lobster meat. Place one mushroom cap on remaining two sides. Ladle over 4-5 ounces of mornay sauce. Cover each casserole completely with a thin layer of the seasoned bread crumbs.

Bake for 15-20 minutes for individual casseroles—sauce should be bubbling. Allow about 10 minutes more if using one large casserole dish. Yield: 6 servings.

From:

**Brandywine
Pub and Food**
2125 Horton Road
Jackson, Michigan

Betty's Meat Pie

This was my mother's recipe.

1 pound ground round
   or chuck
½ pound ground pork
½ cup chopped onion
3 cups shredded potato
1½ cups shredded carrot
1 teaspoon salt
1 teaspoon garlic salt
3 teaspoons seasoned salt
1 tablespoon parsley flakes
2 tablespoons Worcestershire
   sauce
Pastry for 2 9″ double crust pies.

Mix all the ingredients together until well blended.

Preheat oven to 350 degrees. Roll out pastry and line 2 pans. Divide the meat mixture evenly between the 2 pans. Dot tops with 2 tablespoons of butter for each pie. Top with pastry and pinch edges to seal. Cut or slash vents in top pastry crust.

Bake for 1 hour and 15 minutes or until brown and bubbly. Serve with a fresh green salad. Yield: 2 9″ pies—should serve 6.

From: **The Swedish Pantry**
          916 Ludington Street
          Escanaba, Michigan

Quail Saute with Wild Mushrooms and Vegetables
Mustard Vinaigrette

4 quail, boned
4 ounces fiddlehead ferns
20 morels
2 ounces wild leeks
3 ounces shitake mushrooms
8 asparagus spears, peeled
  and cooked till crisp
3 ounces oyster mushrooms
12 cherry tomatoes, cut in half

Mustard Vinaigrette:
2 tablespoons Dijon mustard
½ tablespoon champagne vinegar
1½ tablespoons honey
salt and pepper to taste
4 ounces olive oil

For vinaigrette mix all ingredients but olive oil together well. Then slowly add olive oil while whipping vigorously, adjust seasoning, keep at room temperature.

Saute quail in a little butter, rare. Set aside and keep warm.

Remove green from leeks. Chop both but keep separate. In frying pan with a little butter, saute all vegetables and mushrooms, except cherry tomatoes. When juices start coming out of the mushrooms, add half of the vinaigrette. Toss for 1½ minutes, then add cherry tomatoes and toss until cherry tomatoes are just heated, about 1-2 minutes. Add remainder of vinaigrette, toss gently.

Divide vegetables up evenly on four plates, just scattering them around the plate. Place quail in center of plate and serve.

From: **Justine**
5010 Bay City Road
Midland, Michigan

Scamorza

2 slices Italian bread
1 slice mozzarella
1 slice proscuitto
flour

Egg wash:
2 eggs, beaten
grated Parmesan cheese
parsley, finely chopped

4 tablespoons butter
½ teaspoon capers
1 tablespoon lemon juice

Make a sandwich with the bread, proscuitto and mozzarella. Dust lightly with flour. Dip in egg wash.

In a small skillet, saute the sandwich until golden in olive oil. Remove and keep warm.

Melt butter, stir in lemon juice and add capers, reduce slightly. Keep on stirring until a nice creamy appearance is achieved. Pour over sandwich and serve. Yield: 1-2 servings, for 6 simply triple everything.

From: **Antonio's Restaurant**
20311 Mack Avenue
Grosse Pointe Woods, Michigan

Skillet Penne Tuscan Style

2 cups penne
½ pound sweet Italian
   sausage with fennel
⅓ cup fruity olive oil
1½ cups chopped onion
1½ cups chopped sweet red
   peppers
1 tablespoon minced garlic
½ teaspoon salt
½ teaspoon black pepper
1 tablespoon fresh sage or
   1 teaspoon dried
¼ teaspoon red pepper
   flakes
2 cups canned whole
   tomatoes
½ cup dry vermouth

Bring 2 quarts of water to a boil, add penne and boil until half done or about 8 minutes. (If cooking ahead, drain, chill completely under cold water to stop the cooking process). Set aside.

In an 8-10" frying pan brown the Italian sausage in the olive oil. Add onion and chopped red peppers and cook over medium heat until the vegetables are just tender and the onions are lightly golden. Remove the sausage and cut into ½" slices, then return the slices to the vegetables and add all the ingredients (except the pasta). Cook until the liquid has been reduced to half and then add the cooked pasta and saute, stirring occasionally until all the liquid has been absorbed into the pasta and the oil begins to crackle in the bottom of the pan.

Serve in the skillet garnished with fresh minced parsley or strips of fresh basil leaves. Freshly grated Parmesan should be available on the side. Yield: 6 servings.

From: **Tosi's**
4337 Ridge Road
Stevensville, Michigan

Spinach and Feta Cheese Sandwiches

1 pound frozen, chopped spinach
¾ pound feta cheese, crumbled
1 egg
1 package frozen puff
   pastry dough

Thaw the frozen spinach. Press out of it as much water as possible, then chop finely. Put it into the bowl of an electric mixer with the crumbled feta cheese and the egg, and mix on slow speed just until ingredients are evenly incorporated.

Thaw the dough and roll out to ⅛" thickness. Cut into pieces 3" x 5" with a *very sharp* knife (this allows the pastry to puff more by not sealing the edges). Put ⅓ cup filling in the middle of every other piece.

With a moist pastry brush, carefully paint around the edges of the pieces holding the filling, being careful not to let the water run down the edge of the dough piece. Place a second piece of dough over the filling, and press around the edges to seal it to the bottom piece. Make cuts on an angle through the top dough piece with a very sharp knife or razor blade. Place on a baking sheet about 2" apart and refrigerate for 1 hour.

Preheat oven to 400 degrees. Remove sandwiches from refrigerator and paint their tops with lightly beaten egg white. Again be careful not to let the liquid run down the edges of the pastry. Bake 40-45 minutes or until puffed and brown.

These sandwiches freeze very well and can be baked without thawing with a slight increase in baking time.

From: **Sarkozy's
Bakery and Cafe**
335 Burdick Street
Kalamazoo, Michigan

Spinach Fettucine and Linguine
with Fresh Tomato Sauce

Fresh Tomato Sauce:
4 medium tomatoes,
   peeled, seeded & chopped
½ teaspoon salt
½ teaspoon freshly ground pepper
¼ cup leeks, finely chopped
¾ cup good olive oil
1 tablespoon pesto
½ teaspoon oregano
½ teaspoon lemon juice

Pasta Ingredients:
¼ pound diced bacon
8 ounces spinach fettucine
6 ounces linguine
¼ cup good olive oil
2½ cups broccoli florets
¾ cup zucchini rounds,
   thinly sliced
1¼ cups fresh mushrooms,
   sliced
20 trimmed snow peas
1 cup finely slivered
   fresh spinach
1¾ cups diced mozzarella
1-1½ cups freshly grated
   Parmesan cheese
¾ cup chopped ripe tomatoes

Mix all sauce ingredients together in a large bowl.

Fry bacon until crisp. Drain well and keep warm.

Cook pasta until al dente.

In a large skillet, heat ¼ cup olive oil and saute the broccoli for 2-3 minutes. Do not overcook.

Add zucchini, mushrooms and snow peas and saute until crisp tender.

Add fresh tomato sauce and heat only until sauce is hot—it is important not to cook the sauce.

In a large bowl, toss all ingredients from the skillet with the hot pasta, fresh spinach, mozzarella and bacon.

Serve hot and garnish with a generous sprinkling of freshly grated Parmesan cheese and in center of pasta, place 1 heaping tablespoon of fresh tomato. Offer ground pepper and additional grated Parmesan cheese if desired. Yield: 6 entree portions or 12 first course servings.

From: **The Hearthstone**
3550 Glade (Corner House Motel)
Muskegon, Michigan

Tagliatelle con Dadi di Proscuitto

4 ounces vegetable oil
1 slice proscuitto fat
1 very large onion, chopped
4 tablespoons proscuitto
1 tablespoon basil
24 ounces of Italian tomatoes, peeled
salt and pepper to taste

Put the vegetable oil in a pan over medium heat. Add the slice of proscuitto fat and cook until browned. Return to heat.

When onions are brown, add chopped proscuitto and basil and mix on the heat for 5-10 seconds. Add tomatoes and salt and pepper to taste. Bring to a boil and cook until it reaches desired thickness. Yield: 6 servings.

From: **Antonio's Restaurant**
20311 Mack Avenue
Grosse Pointe Woods, Michigan

Tofu Teriyaki

Sauce:
2 cups water
½ cup tamari*
¾ cup pineapple juice
6 tablespoons saki*
2 tablespoons honey
2 tablespoons rice vinegar
4 cloves garlic, minced
1 tablespoon grated ginger

¼ cup water
4 tablespoons arrowroot

Vegetables:
2 cups bok choy, sliced
2 cups green onions, sliced
*   in 2" lengths*
2 cups sliced red pepper
2 cups pea pods, trimmed
2 cups sliced mushrooms

1 pound tofu, cut in 1" chunks
½ pound mung sprouts

*Tamari is fermented soy sauce available in Oriental specialty stores or the Oriental section of good supermarkets. Saki is Japanese wine made from rice.

Bring all the sauce ingredients to a boil except the ¼ cup water and arrowroot. Whisk the arrowroot and water together in a bowl and add to the sauce, cooking until thick, stirring occasionally.

Cut up all the vegetables and mix together. Cut up the tofu.

Stir fry in a large wok, beginning with the tofu, adding the vegetables and finally the mung sprouts, just before serving. Serve over rice with sauce on top. Yield: 8 servings.

From: **Seva Restaurant**
314 East Liberty Street
Ann Arbor, Michigan

Bread, Rolls, Muffins

Bread, Rolls, Muffins

Whole books have been written on bread and rightly so; it is an important part of the human diet. It is also a widely varied source of food—it is amazing what you can add to the basic ingredients to differ the taste and texture and still come out with something wonderful and edible.

Michigan's chefs have not only realized this, but have incorporated some of their best known local produce into the process—there is Morel Beer Bread in this chapter. There are also interesting variations on old themes—how do rum raisin oatmeal cookies sound? Adult cookies, perhaps. Or gingerbread muffins?

We have also included a recipe for injera, the bread of Ethiopia, necessary if you are to eat Ethiopian food. And since we have recipes for other Ethiopian dishes in the book, we have included the bread here.

There are also some traditional favorites that you love and may have wanted to try for yourself. Swedish Rye and Boston Brown Bread are good examples. Good luck and good leavening.

Baked Boston Brown Bread

2½ cups brown sugar
1 quart buttermilk
  or sour milk
4 cups all-bran
4 cups flour
4 teaspoons baking soda
2 teaspoons salt
2 cups raisins

Preheat oven to 350 degrees.

Mix together the brown sugar and buttermilk, stirring well to blend thoroughly.

Add in the flour, all-bran, soda, salt and raisins. Mix well and put in well greased loaf tins. Bake for 50-60 minutes or until a toothpick inserted in center of loaf comes out clean. Yield: 2 large loaves

From:

**The Shaker
Good Room**
406 West Savidge
Spring Lake, Michigan

Injera

This recipe produces a close approximation to injera, the national bread of Ethiopia.

To make about 6 9″ rounds:
¼ cup all purpose flour
2 teaspoons baking powder
½ teaspoon salt
¼ cup lemon juice
⅔ cup water
1 can club soda or beer
  at room temperature

Combine the flour, salt, baking powder and lemon juice in a deep bowl. Stirring constantly with a whisk or spoon, pour in the water and beer or club soda in a slow stream, and continue to stir until the mixture is a smooth, thin cream. Strain the batter through a fine sieve set over a clean bowl, pressing down hard on any lumps with the back of a spoon.

Cook the injera in a 10" skillet or omelet pan with a nonstick surface or a well-seasoned cast iron skillet. Warm the ungreased pan over moderate heat until it is just hot enough to set the batter without browning it. To test the heat, pour 1 tablespoon of the batter into the center of the pan. The bottom surface should solidify immediately, without becoming brown.

For each injera, remove the pan from the heat and ladle in a ¼ cup of batter. Then quickly tip the pan back and forth to cover the bottom evenly. Cook the injera over a moderate heat for 1 minute, or just until the top is spongy, moist and dotted with tiny air holes. The bottom should be smooth, dry and somewhat shiny. Do not let the bottom brown, otherwise the edges may become too crisp. Remove the pan from the heat, and using a spatula or your fingers, lift the injera gently out of the pan. Lay it on a plate to cool. Wipe the pan with a clean cloth, and ladle another ¼ cup of the batter into the pan. Repeat the process and when the next injera is done, transfer the cooled one to a serving platter and place the hot one on the plate to cool.

To serve, spread three or four injera in a shallow, flat basket, letting them overlap and drape over the edges. Fold the rest into quarters and arrange them attractively in the center.

From: **The Blue Nile**
Trapper's Alley
508 Monroe Street
Detroit, Michigan

Morel and Beer Bread

1 ounce dried morels
12 ounces beer
½ cup warm water
½ ounce dry yeast
1 teaspoon sugar
2½ cups unbleached flour
1¾ cups cake flour
2 teaspoons salt
cornmeal

Heat beer in small saucepan and add the morels which you have ground in a coffee mill. Let this mixture cool to about 90 degrees. Meanwhile, proof the yeast with the warm water and sugar for about 10 minutes. In a large bowl, mix the flour together with the salt, and add the yeast and beer mixtures. Stir the mixture until well combined and smooth. The dough should be elastic and spongy and quite wet. Place dough in large greased ceramic bowl, turning dough so it is completely coated. Cover the bowl with plastic wrap, and place in a warm place, till the dough has doubled, about one hour.

Preheat the oven to 450 degrees. Place the dough on a heavily floured board, working enough flour into the dough so it can be handled easily and is no longer sticky. Work the dough into a ball, and place in a bowl or pan lined with a well floured cloth. cover with a piece of well oiled plastic wrap, let rise in a warm place until almost double, about 30-40 minutes. Sprinkle cornmeal on an oiled cookie sheet and invert the dough onto the sheet. Slash the dough as desired and bake in oven for 20 minutes; reduce the oven temperature to 400 degrees and bake 10 minutes longer, until bread is brown and sounds hollow when tapped. Yield: 1 loaf.

From:

Tapawingo
9502 Lake Street
Ellsworth, Michigan

Potato Caraway Bread

1¾ cups water
1 package compressed
    yeast
1 cup mashed potatoes
1 tablespoon salt
1 tablespoon caraway
    seeds
6¼ cups flour

Put the water, yeast and mashed potatoes in mixing bowl and mix slowly until yeast is dissolved. Add salt and caraway seed. Add the flour in stages and mix well, using the dough hook on your mixer, if you have one.

Remove the dough from the mixing bowl and continue kneading it for 10 more minutes. Place the dough in a buttered bowl, turning the dough to coat it. Cover with a clean cloth, and allow to rise in a warm place until double in bulk.

Divide the dough in half. For each half, flatten or roll out to a square approximately 12" x 12". Roll up the piece from one edge as lightly as possible. Seal the seam and ends.

Preheat oven to 400 degrees. Place both loaves on a lightly greased cookie sheet covered with cornmeal and allow to rise until about doubled.

When risen, paint each loaf with water and make four diagonal cuts in the top of each loaf. Place in oven and bake for 40 minutes or until nicely browned. Yield: 2 loaves.

From:

**Sarkozy's
Bakery and Cafe**
335 North Burdick Street
Kalamazoo, Michigan

Swedish Rye Bread

2 tablespoons dry yeast
¼ cup warm water
1 teaspoon sugar
1 cup evaporated milk
3 cups water
2 tablespoons shortening
1 cup sugar
1 cup molasses
1 tablespoon salt
3 cups rye flour
9 cups white flour

Dissolve the yeast in the warm water with the teaspoon of sugar. Water should be about 110 degrees.

Combine the milk and water. Scald and cool. Add the shortening, sugar, molasses, and salt, mixing well.

Beat in the rye flour a ½ cup at a time. Then add the white flour gradually, mixing with a wooden spoon, until thick. Knead in the remainder of the flour until the dough is no longer sticky. Place in a well greased bowl, turn the dough to coat thoroughly. Cover with a clean towel and let rise in a warm, draft-free place until double in bulk.

Punch down and divide the dough into 4 equal pieces. Roll each out into a rectangle, roll up to form a loaf, pinch ends of dough together and place in a well greased 9" x 4" loaf pan.

Preheat oven to 350 degrees while dough rises again. When dough has doubled, place in oven and bake for 40-45 minutes until loaves are well browned and sound hollow when rapped with a knuckle. Yield: 4 loaves.

This bread is delicious for sandwiches or toast. This bread is not difficult to make and the aroma when baking is heavenly. Everyone should make bread once in their lives.

From: **The Swedish Pantry**
819 Ludington Street
Escanaba, Michigan

Coconut Muffins

½ cup butter, melted
¾ cup honey
3 eggs
¾ cup buttermilk
3 cups whole wheat
  pastry flour
1½ teaspoons baking
  powder
¾ teaspoon baking soda
1½ cups shredded,
  unsweetened coconut

Preheat oven to 350 degrees. Grease muffin tins well, or line with paper cups.

Whisk together the butter, honey, eggs and buttermilk until well blended. Sift together the dry ingredients in a separate bowl.

Toss coconut into dry ingredients, mix. Add the wet ingredients to the dry ingredients, mixing gently until just blended. It is important not to overmix muffins. Put into muffin tins and place in the oven. Bake for 25-30 minutes or until a toothpick inserted in the center of a muffin comes out clean. Cool for a few minutes in pan, then remove to a basket lined with a linen napkin or clean towel to keep warm until you eat them all. Yield: 1 dozen muffins.

From: **Seva Restaurant**
314 East Liberty
Ann Arbor, Michigan

Gingerbread Muffins

6 tablespoons butter
2 tablespoons freshly
  grated ginger, packed
½ cup molasses
¼ cup honey
1 cup buttermilk
3 eggs
3 cups whole wheat
  pastry flour
1½ teaspoons baking powder

Simmer the butter and ground ginger together over very low heat for 20 minutes. Whisk together the molasses, honey, buttermilk, eggs and ginger/butter mixture until well blended.

Preheat the oven to 350 degrees. Grease muffin tins or line with paper muffin cups. Sift the dry ingredients together in a separate bowl. Add in the raisins, tossing to mix well.

¾ teaspoon baking soda
1 teaspoon dry mustard
¾ teaspoon ground
   cloves
¾ teaspoon cinnamon
½ teaspoon nutmeg
1 cup raisins

Add the dry ingredients to the wet ingredients, mixing gently until just blended. Bake in the oven for 25-30 minutes until muffins are nicely browned and a toothpick inserted in the center comes out clean.

Cool for a few minutes in the pan, then remove muffins to a basket lined with a clean cloth napkin or towel to keep them warm. Enjoy! Yield: 1 dozen muffins.

From: **Seva Restaurant**
314 East Liberty Street
Ann Arbor, Michigan

Lemon Coconut Muffins

8 cups flour
2½ cups sugar
1 tablespoon plus
   1 teaspoon baking powder
1 teaspoon salt
4 eggs, beaten
1 cup melted butter
3½ cups milk
½ cup lemon juice
1 tablespoon lemon
   zest, grated
¼ teaspoon orange
   zest, grated
1¼ cups unsweetened
   coconut, shredded

Preheat oven to 375 degrees. Sift together the dry ingredients and add coconut, lemon zest, orange zest to the dry mixture. Mix eggs, milk and butter. Add the lemon juice last, stirring quickly to prevent curdling. Make a well in the center of the dry ingredients and stir in the egg mixture. Be careful not to overmix, stir just enough to mix thoroughly. Spoon into greased muffin tins. Bake for 30-35 minutes or until toothpick inserted in center of muffin comes out clean. Yield: 24-28 large muffins.

From: **A Slice of Heaven**
116 South Main Street
Ann Arbor, Michigan

Lucille Killeen's Potato Doughnuts

⅞ cup water
½ cup plus
   1 tablespoon sugar
⅞ cup mashed potato
2 packages compressed
   yeast
3 eggs
1 tablespoon salt
½ cup vegatable oil
6 cups flour
peanut oil for frying

Place water, yeast, sugar, salt and mashed potato in mixing bowl and blend until smooth. Add the eggs and oil and blend well. Add flour in stages and mix dough well, using dough hook on mixer, if available.

Remove dough from mixer and knead well for 15 minutes on a floured board. Roll the dough into a ball and place in a greased bowl, turning dough to coat with oil. Cover and allow to rise until doubled in bulk.

Roll out ½" thick and cut out pieces with doughnut cutter. Place pieces on greased cookie sheet and cover lightly with a towel.

Put 1½" peanut oil in a deep frying pan and heat to 375 degrees. Use a candy thermometer for this stage, as frying fat less than 375 degrees will yield greasy doughnuts and more than 375 degrees will yield doughnuts that brown before they are done on the inside.

With a spatula, remove the risen doughnuts from the cookie sheet and lower them one at a time into the hot fat. Allow to fry about 2 minutes on a side. These doughnuts will brown quickly and will be darker than the average yeast doughnut when done. Remove from the fat and put on paper towels to cool. While still warm, dredge in cinnamon sugar, or wait until cool and dredge in powdered sugar. Yield: approximately 12 doughnuts.

From:
**Sarkozy's
Bakery and Cafe**
335 North Burdick Street
Kalamazoo, Michigan

Rum Raisin Oatmeal Cookies

½ cup dark rum
1 cup water
1 pound butter, softened
1 pound brown sugar
4 eggs, beaten
3 cups unbleached flour
2 teaspoons salt
2 teaspoons baking powder
1 teaspoon vanilla
   extract
1 teaspoon dark rum
2 cups walnut pieces
6 cups rolled oats
1 pound white raisins

Heat the rum and water in a saucepan, just until hot. Pour over raisins in a bowl and let soften.

Preheat oven to 350 degrees. Grease cookie sheets.

In a mixer, beat the butter until creamy. Scrape sides and bottom often, beating 5-10 minutes. Add brown sugar to the creamed butter. Beat until light and fluffy. Scrape sides and bottom of bowl. With mixer on low, add the slightly beaten eggs. Again, scrape the sides and bottom of bowl. Turn on medium speed and beat for 3 minutes. Add the vanilla and rum. Turn mixer back to low and add flour, salt and baking powder a little at a time, scraping sides and bottom of bowl. Add the rolled oats and then the walnuts. Mix. Strain the rum water from the raisins and add the raisins. (You can save rum water for the next batch.)

Beat just until everything is combined. Scoop with ice cream scoop and flatten out with wet hands. Leave plenty of room as they will flatten out. Bake for 20-25 minutes. Yield: approximately 4 dozen cookies.

From: **A Slice of Heaven**
116 South Main Street
Ann Arbor, Michigan

Father Christmas Butter Shortbread Cookies

1 cup butter
½ cup sugar
1 egg
3 teaspoons vanilla
   extract
3 cups flour
½ teaspoon baking powder

Cream the butter, sugar and egg together well. Sift in flour and baking powder. Mix well. Chill dough thoroughly.

Preheat oven to 425 degrees. Roll out dough to ¼" thickness. Cut with antique cookie cutters. Place on cookie sheet and decorate with currants, raisins, slivered almonds, etc. Bake in oven for 5-7 minutes. The number of cookies depends on the size of the cutters.

From: **The Victorian Villa**
601 North Broadway Street
Union City, Michigan

Appetizers

Appetizers

An appetizer is defined as something to whet the appetite, to heighten the anticipation of the meal to follow. Certainly Michigan's restaurateurs and chefs understand this as well as anyone.

Some restaurants are encouraging their clientele to order a variety of "small plates" or appetizers, rather than a several course meal. This seems to be in response to a demand for light, delectable food because people are eating out more than ever before. Because they do, they want food that's relatively quick and won't break either the bank or the belt. Appetizers, for that reason, are becoming more varied and more interesting.

There are appetizers here to tempt the finickiest appetite. There are dishes here that are so wonderful it is easy to make a meal of them and forget the rest. See if you don't agree. Michigan chefs know how to tempt the appetite.

Artichoke Hearts Grande Mere

1 cup crabmeat
¾ cup dill sauce
1 can artichoke hearts

Dill Sauce:
1 clove garlic, minced
¼ cup chopped chives
2 tablespoons chopped parsley
½ teaspoon salt
¼ teaspoon pepper
¼ cup dill weed
¼ cup fresh lemon juice
1 cup mayonnaise,
   preferably homemade
½ cup sour cream

Mix all the ingredients for the dill sauce together and chill thoroughly.

Add ¾ cup of the dill sauce to the crabmeat. Trim the bottoms of the artichoke hearts so that they sit evenly. Remove some of the leaves of the heart and fill with the crab mixture.

Arrange 2-3 stuffed artichokes on each plate, which you have lined with leaf lettuce. On each artichoke heart place a spoonful of the dill sauce and garnish with lemon and tomato slices. Yield: 3-4 servings.

From: **Grande Mere Inn**
5800 Red Arrow Highway
Stevensville, Michigan

Artichoke Hearts
with Escargots, Spinach and Crabmeat Sauce Mornay

*1 quart Mornay sauce**
12 artichokes
1 pound fresh spinach,
  cleaned and blanched
  (to yield 1 cup)
72 large snails, rinsed
1 pound lump crabmeat
1 cup white wine
1 teaspoon shallots
1 teaspoon fresh garlic
1 teaspoon vinegar
1 bunch fresh tarragon
salt and pepper to taste
Old Bay seasoning to taste

**"The Joy of Cooking" contains a good recipe for Mornay sauce.*

To prepare the artichokes, blanch in boiling, salted water until completely done, approximately 15 minutes. Then shock in a mixture of cold water and vinegar. Remove tough outer leaves. Trim tops of leaves remaining. Cut artichoke in half lengthwise. Remove choke, creating a natural well for stuffing.

Pick over crabmeat carefully to remove any membranes.

Saute the garlic and shallots in a little butter and olive oil. Add snails and toss to coat snails. Add the wine and cook down to a glaze. Cool and add the tarragon, reserving 12 sprigs for garnish.

Mix the blanched spinach with enough Mornay sauce to just bind, reserving the rest of the sauce.

Preheat oven to 375 degrees. To assemble, place artichokes in a baking pan. In the well of each, place 3 of the snails, add spinach mixture, top with crabmeat. Ladle Mornay sauce over top, still reserving some for serving.

Bake for 15 minutes. Cover the bottom of each serving plate with Mornay sauce. Place 2 artichokes in middle of plate, garnish with tarragon sprig and serve. Yield: 12 servings.

From: **The Whitney**
4421 Woodward Avenue
Detroit, Michigan

Baked Artichokes Filled with Chevre

12 medium artichokes
4 ounces chevre
  cheese
freshly grated Parmesan
½ cup champagne
¾ cup heavy cream
1 teaspoon shallots
  minced
¼ cup julienne spinach
2 tablespoons butter
¼ cup red peppers,
  finely diced

Cut the stems off the artichokes and trim the tops of the leaves down to the heart. Cook in boiling water with one lemon cut in half to prevent discoloration. Boil for 20 minutes or until barely tender. Remove with a slotted spoon and plunge into ice water. When cool, use a teaspoon to carefully remove the hairy choke portion.

Preheat oven to 400 degrees. Fill the artichoke hearts with the chevre and dust the tops with the Parmesan cheese. Bake for 7 minutes.

While artichokes are baking, make the sauce. Reduce the champagne by half over medium heat. Add heavy cream, shallots, reduce by one quarter. Add the butter, spinach, and red peppers. Season to taste.

Spoon champagne sauce evenly onto four 5" plates and place three artichokes on each plate and serve. Yield: 4 servings.

From: **Cafe Le Chat**
17001 Kercheval
Grosse Pointe, Michigan

Carrot and
Green Bean Terrine

1 pound, 6 ounces carrots,
    julienne
1 pound, 6 ounces green beans

Custard:
6 eggs
¼ teaspoon white pepper
½ teaspoon dill weed
½ teaspoon garlic,
    minced
¾ teaspoon salt
1½ cups milk

Preheat oven to 325 degrees. Peel carrots and cut in julienne strips about ¼" thick. Parboil then plunge in cold water. Remove stem ends from green beans then parboil, plunging in cold water.

Butter a 9 x 5 x 3½" bread pan. Cut a piece of parchment paper to fit the bottom of the bread pan.

Layer the vegetables all the way to the top of the pan—1 layer of beans, 1 layer of carrots and so on to the top. Lightly press them to settle them in.

Mix together all the custard ingredients, beating well to blend thoroughly.

Pour the custard over the layered vegetables and let it settle in.

Put the bread pan in another pan with water coming halfway up the sides of the bread pan. Bake for 2½ hours. The terrine should break apart in the center when split with a knife.

Cool terrine for ½ hour before unmolding. To unmold, place a plate or flat pan over the bread pan, then flip both over, lightly tapping the sides and bottom of the bread pan to loosen the terrine.

Use a large knife, cut in ¾" slices to serve. Yield: 10-12 servings.

From:

**MacKinnon's
of Northville**
126-130 East Main Street
Northville, Michigan

The Ample Cheese Cracker

½ cup butter
½ pound sharp cheddar
cheese, grated
1 cup flour
⅓ package onion soup mix
½ teaspoon salt

Let butter and cheese come to room temperature and mix thoroughly. Add the remaining ingredients and blend. Shape into three rolls about 1" in diameter. Wrap in wax paper and chill thoroughly,

Preheat oven to 375 degrees. Slice rolls into ¼" slices. Bake on ungreased cookie sheets for 10-12 minutes or until brown around the edges. Store in airtight container. These are best eaten the first day.

From: **The Ample Pantry**
5629 Stadium Drive
Kalamazoo, Michigan

Dilly Dip Spread

2 tablespoons fresh dill
2 tablespoons fresh
parsley
8 ounces cream cheese
4 ounces butter or
margarine
4 ounces sour cream
2 tablespoons fresh
lemon juice
1 tablespoon freshly
ground black pepper
1 teaspoon seasoned salt

In a blender or food processor, mince fresh herbs. Dill and parsley are favorites at The Ample Pantry, but mix your own preference. Fresh herbs are the key. Add the cream cheese, butter and sour cream, which have been brought to room temperature. Blend, then add the rest of the ingredients.

Chill for several hours. Great with all fresh vegetables as a dip. Nice as a spread on specialty fruit breads and wonderful as a spread on sandwiches. Will keep for several days if stored in the refrigerator in a tightly covered container.

From: **The Ample Pantry**
5629 Stadium Drive
Kalamazoo, Michigan

Lamb Curry Hors d'Oeuvres

1¼ pound ground lamb
salt and pepper to taste
1 small onion, diced
1 tablespoon curry powder
1 teaspoon ground cumin
2 cloves garlic, minced
1 teaspoon basil
1 teaspoon oregano
puff pastry sheets

Saute the lamb in a heavy skillet for 10 minutes. Drain off any grease, leaving about 1 tablespoonful.

Remove lamb and saute onion in same pan until soft. Return lamb to the pan and add the other seasonings. Saute about another 10 minutes. Cool slightly and coarsely chop in food processor to obtain a homogeneous consistency.

Preheat oven to 425 degrees. Cut out puff pastry rounds about 3" in diameter. Brush with water and place 1 teaspoon of lamb filling on each round. Fold over and seal with a fork. Chill until firm, or freeze until needed. Bake for 30 minutes, or until brown.

From: **The Moveable Feast**
326 West Liberty Street
Ann Arbor, Michigan

Morels over Angel Hair Pasta

2 tablespoons butter
1½ cups morels, cleaned
1 tablespoon shallots, minced
¼ cup sherry
¼ cup veal stock
1¼ cups heavy cream
2 cups angel hair pasta, cooked
1 teaspoon fresh thyme
1½ tablespoons minced
  fresh chives

In a heavy saucepan melt the butter. Add the morels, which you have cleaned carefully and cut in half, with the shallots. Saute until soft. Add sherry and veal stock and reduce over high heat until almost evaporated.

Add the cream and reduce by half. Add the pasta, thyme and chives, tossing until heated through.

Divide onto 6 warmed appetizer plates. Garnish with julienne of fresh tomato and thyme sprigs. Yield: 6 portions.

From: **The Money Tree**
333 West Fort Street
Detroit, Michigan

Orange Pecan Puff Pastry Tart

6 ounces pecans
2 tablespoons butter
¾ pound cream cheese
6 ounces bleu cheese
½ cup parsley, chopped
1 tablespoon grated orange
   zest
puff pastry, homemade
   or purchased

Saute pecan pieces in the butter until golden brown, about 5-10 minutes. Beat the cream cheese, which has been allowed to soften, with the bleu cheese until fluffy. Add orange zest and the pecans. Beat until just mixed or about 2 minutes.

Working quickly in a cool area, spread one sheet of pastry out and poke all over with a fork. Place on a baking sheet lined with parchment paper. Brush the outer edges with water. Cut strips ½" wide and as long as the sheet of puff pastry. Press them to the outside edges, which you have brushed with water, to form a border. Then cut 2 more strips ½" wide and as long as the width of the pastry sheet. Press them to the outside edges and over the other border.

Brush with egg wash, carefully, not dripping any on the sides, or it will prevent the pastry from puffing. Chill until thoroughly cold.

Preheat oven to 375 degrees. Bake the pastry in the oven until puffed and golden, approximately 15 minutes.

Remove from the oven and spoon the filling into the center, spreading evenly inside the border. Bake again for 10-15 minutes, just until filling lightly browns. Cool slightly and serve. Cut into squares to serve.

From: **A Slice of Heaven**
113 South Main Street
Ann Arbor, Michigan

Pear D'Anjou
with Prosciutto and Gorgonzola en Croute

6 Anjou pears, medium size
½ cup Gorgonzola
   cheese
¼ cup cream cheese
2 ounces prosciutto,
   sliced thin and minced
cracked pepper to taste
1 package frozen puff
   pastry
2 eggs, beaten

Preheat the oven to 350 degrees. Using an apple corer or melon baller, core the Anjou pears.

In a medium sized mixing bowl, cream the Gorgonzola and cream cheese together. Add the prosciutto and the freshly cracked pepper; blend thoroughly.

Using a pastry bag with a large round tip, fill pears with the Gorgonzola mixture.

Roll the thawed puff pastry sheets out on a floured board, till it is ⅛" thick. Cut in 3 equal portions. Repeat for the other puff pastry sheets.

Wrap each pear in the puff pastry sheets. Form the pastry so that it is shaped like the pear. Close the seams with some of the beaten egg. Coat the entire pastry with the egg wash.

Bake for 30 minutes or until the pastry is golden brown. Yield: 6 portions.

From: **South Street Culinary Shoppe**
116 West South Street
Kalamazoo, Michigan

Garlic Potato Crepe
with Backfin Crabmeat, Crayfish and American Sturgeon Caviar and Chive Butter

Crepe Batter:
1 whole garlic bulb, roasted
  at 425 degrees until tender,
  then peeled while warm
½ pound peeled new potatoes,
  cooked until tender
1 cup milk
2½ tablespoons heavy cream
2½ tablespoons flour
2 whole eggs plus
  2 egg whites
salt, pepper and
  nutmeg to taste

Sauce:
1 cup white wine
4 ounces shallots, sliced
½ cup heavy cream
12 ounces butter
2 ounces chives, cut
  into ½" pieces
salt, pepper, tabasco and
  red wine vinegar to taste

9 ounces Maryland backfin
  crabmeat, picked over
48 live crayfish, poached in
  salted water for 10 seconds
6 ounces American sturgeon
  caviar
1 ounce unsalted butter

In a food processor, purée garlic and potatoes together, then add milk and flour. Next add eggs, egg whites and heavy cream. Season with salt, pepper, and nutmeg. Blend mixture to avoid any lumps. Place in a container and leave at room temperature while you make the sauce.

In a heavy saucepan, put the white wine and shallots and reduce the wine to a glaze. Add cream, reduce down until cream becomes a light yellow color. Then cut the butter in small pieces and add a little at a time, beating constantly over low heat. When all the butter has been incorporated, season with salt, pepper, tabasco and red wine vinegar. This sauce must not boil after the butter has been added. Then add the chives and keep the sauce warm, but not hot or it will break.

Using a crepe pan or cast iron skillet, heat pan over medium heat with butter until a drop of batter hisses or spits. Ladle 1 ounce or so of batter into the center of pan, tilting slightly to form crepe. Cook for several seconds on one side until golden brown, then flip and cook on other side until golden brown. Remove to a cookie sheet and keep warm.

Saute crabmeat and crayfish quickly in butter, tossing gently not to break up crabmeat. Season with salt and pepper. Then fill each crepe with mixture, dividing crabmeat and crayfish evenly. Place two crepes on each plate, with sauce around them, top with ½ ounce each of American sturgeon caviar. May be garnished with crayfish bodies if desired.

From: **Justine**
5010 Bay City Road
Midland, Michigan

Smoked Whitefish Cheesecake

2 tablespoons butter
¾ cup bread crumbs
½ cup Parmesan cheese
½ teaspoon fresh dill

4½ tablespoons butter
2½ pound cream cheese
6 eggs
¾ cup grated soft white cheese
½ cup half & half
½ teaspoon salt
½ teaspoon white pepper
¾ pound smoked whitefish

Blend these ingredients in a food processor or blender and sprinkle in a 10" springform pan.

Preheat oven to 325 degrees. In a food processor, blend together the butter, the cream cheese, which has been allowed to soften, the eggs, white cheese, half & half, salt and pepper. When thoroughly blended, add the onion and the smoked whitefish, after you have removed the skin and bones.

Pour batter into prepared pan and wrap bottom with aluminum foil. Place pan in a larger pan with enough hot water to come half way up the side. Bake for about 1½ hours. Then turn off oven and let it sit for another hour. Chill well before slicing.

From: **The Rowe Inn**
County Road C48
Ellsworth, Michigan

Soups

Soups

Soup is such a universal dish, it is served in so many countries, so many cultures, that you would think the subject would have been exhausted long ago, culinarily speaking. As this chapter shows, Michigan's chefs have found new ways to make soup different, interesting and enticing at the same time.

This chapter is almost a book in itself, there are so many new ways with old ingredients. There are new variations on the old seafood chowders; there are new vegetable soups; new ways of using potatoes in soup. . . but see and taste for yourself.

Soup is also a dish that bespeaks home as few other things do. On a cold, wet, wintry day there are few things more comforting than a bowl of hot, homemade soup.

And for sheer elegance on a too warm summer evening, it's hard to beat a chilled soup. So it's versatile as well as universal. Here's to soup and, in particular, Michigan's soups.

Apple Cider Soup
with Cinnamon Dumplings

Soup:
½ cup diced onion
½ cup diced carrot
1 clove garlic
3 apples, peeled
   and cored
3 tablespoons butter
2-3 tablespoons flour
1 quart apple cider
juice of 1 lemon
½ teaspoon each nutmeg,
   cinnamon and white pepper

Dumplings:
2 tablespoons butter
2 eggs
6 tablespoons flour
1 tablespoon onion, minced
¼ teaspoon salt
¼ teaspoon cinnamon

In a saucepan, saute the onions, carrots, garlic and apples until soft. Add the flour and stir. Add cider slowly, stirring to blend, then cover and simmer for 20 minutes. Transfer to a food processor or blender and puree. Add seasonings, taste and adjust as necessary. Return to the pan and bring to a simmer.

Meanwhile, beat the butter until soft. Beat and add the egg. Stir in the rest of the ingredients for the dumplings. Drop the batter into the simmering liquid using a spoon. Cover the pan and simmer for about 7 minutes. Ladle into bowls and garnish with cinnamon sticks.

From: **The Rowe Inn**
County Road 48
Ellsworth, Michigan

Asparagus Vicyhssoise

2 strips bacon, chopped
2 ounces clarified butter
1 onion, chopped
1 rib celery, chopped
1 carrot, chopped
1 leek, chopped
1 potato, chopped
pepper to taste
2 ounces flour
2 quarts liquid (stock or water,
    chicken bouillon to taste)
1 pound asparagus
8 ounces sour cream
4 ounces half & half cream

Cook the bacon in the butter. Add the chopped vegetables. Let simmer for 10 minutes, stirring occasionally. Add flour, then add liquid. Simmer for 45 minutes. Add asparagus. Simmer for another 7 minutes.

Puree in blender or food processor. Add the sour cream and half & half. Chill thoroughly.

From: **Oakley's
at the Haymarket**
161 East Michigan Avenue
Kalamazoo, Michigan

Bay Pointe Chowder

2 tablespoons butter
½ cup diced celery
½ cup diced onion
½ cup diced carrots
¼ cup diced tomatoes,
    seeds removed
⅓ pound raw shrimp, diced
⅓ pound raw clams
⅓ pound raw lobster
1 teaspoon paprika
½ cup blanched redskin
    potatoes, diced
1½ ounces cream sherry
1 pint homemade chicken stock
1 quart heavy cream

Melt the 2 tablespoons of butter and combine celery, onions, and carrots. Saute until onions are translucent. Add shrimp, clams and lobster and continue to saute until lightly cooked. Add tomatoes and cream sherry and cook for 3 minutes. Add chicken stock, cream and seasonings. Simmer for 20 minutes.

Combine the melted butter and flour in the roux into a smooth paste and cook over a low heat for 5 minutes.

Raise heat on simmering chowder and add roux, a third at a time, whisking briskly. Simmer for 2-3 minutes each time. After roux is added, stir in redskin potatoes and

1 teaspoon salt
1 teaspoon white pepper
¼ cup fresh lemon juice

Roux:
8 ounces melted butter
⅓ cup flour

simmer soup for 20 minutes. Season to taste and serve immediately. Yield: 6-8 servings.

From: **The Bay Pointe Restaurant**
11456 Marsh Road
Shelbyville, Michigan

Black Bean Soup

1 pound dried black beans
¼ cup olive oil
½ pound salt pork, cut
    into ½" cubes
¼ cup raw, cured ham, cut into
    ½" cubes
¼ cup garlic, finely minced
4 cups finely chopped onions
14 cups beef stock,
    preferably homemade
¼ teaspoon cayenne pepper
2 tablespoons wine vinegar
½ cup dry sherry

chopped onion
thin slices of lime
finely chopped ham*

*A Smithfield or country
    ham is best for this soup.

Rinse the beans well and pick over them to remove any foreign particles. Put the beans in a mixing bowl and add cold water to cover to a depth of about 4" above the beans. Let stand overnight.

Heat the oil in a soup kettle and add the salt pork, cubed ham, onion and garlic. Cook, stirring, about 5 minutes, until onions are translucent and salt pork has been rendered of fat.

Drain the beans well and add them to the kettle. Add the broth and bring to a boil. Add salt and black pepper to taste, and cayenne pepper. Partially cover and cook, stirring occasionally, about 4 hours.

Put half the soup with the beans through a food mill, sieve, or purée in a blender. Return this mixture to the kettle and stir to blend with the remaining soup and beans. Add the vinegar and sherry. Serve piping hot and pass bowls of chopped onion, lime slices, chopped ham and rice for garnish. This soup is excellent when reheated. Yield: 12 servings.

From: **Restaurant Duglass**
29269 Southfield Road
Southfield, Michigan

Sicilian Bean Soup

1 cup navy beans
3 cups water or vegetable
  stock
¼ cup olive oil
4 cloves garlic, minced
1 cup diced onion
½ cup diced celery
½ diced carrot
½ chopped green pepper
1 cup chopped zucchini
3 cups water or vegetable
  stock
1½ teaspoons salt
1 teaspoon oregano
1½ teaspoon basil
1 teaspoon black pepper
3 ounces tomato paste
1 cup sliced black olives
1 tablespoon fresh lemon
  juice

Cook the beans in the water or vegetable stock for 1½ hours over medium low heat. The beans should be tender and not mushy.

Saute the garlic and onions in the olive oil. When onions are translucent, add celery, carrot, green pepper and zucchini.

Add the sauteed vegetables to the beans. Add the additional stock or water and seasonings with the olives and simmer for ½ hour or until flavors have melded.

From: **Seva Restaurant**
          314 East Michigan Avenue
          Ann Arbor, Michigan

Cream of Broccoli Soup

½ cup margarine
1 cup flour
¼ teasoon white pepper
¼ teaspoon nutmeg
2 teaspoons onion flakes
1 quart chicken broth
1 quart whole milk
1 pound cooked, chopped
  broccoli

Melt the margarine in a heavy kettle. Add the flour, white pepper, nutmeg and onion flakes and whisk in. Cook over low heat for 4 minutes. Whisk in the chicken broth and cook until thick and bubbling. Add the whole milk and stir to combine.

Add the broccoli and heat thoroughly, but do not boil.

Fresh, young asparagus may be substituted in season. Delicious! This is our most popular soup.

From: **The Swedish Pantry**
819 Ludington Street
Escanaba, Michigan

Butternut Squash Soup

1 medium butternut squash
½ onion, diced
¼ pound butter
⅞ cup flour
2 quarts chicken stock
1 teaspoon nutmeg
1 teaspoon cinnamon
1 teaspoon mace
white pepper and salt to taste
½ to 1 quart heavy cream

Peel butternut squash and dice. Saute squash and onion in butter until tender. Add flour to form a roux. Cook for 5 minutes, stirring to make sure the roux does not brown. Add chicken stock and bring to a boil and then let simmer for 10-15 minutes. Mix nutmeg, cinnamon, mace, and white pepper with heavy cream and add to the simmering pot. Let simmer for another 10 minutes. Place in food processor or blender and puree for 2 minutes. Strain through a china cap or strainer. Salt and pepper to taste. Yield: 10 servings.

From: **Periwinkle's**
400 West Main Street
Brighton, Michigan

Spicy Cauliflower Soup

1½ cups onions, chopped
1 head cauliflower, broken
    into small pieces
4 cups potatoes, cubed
2-3 tablespoons chili powder
1 teaspoon ground coriander
1½ teaspoons ground cumin
1 tablespoon ground turmeric
1 tablespoon black pepper
1-2 teaspoons salt
1 teaspoon cayenne
2 quarts water
½ cup vinegar
½ cup tamarind concentrate,
    dissolved in hot water*

*Tamarind can be found in food stores that specialize in Indian foods. It comes in small containers of concentrate.

Fry the onions, cauliflower, and spices in just enough hot oil to coat them as they are stirred.

Add water, vinegar, and tamarind liquid. Brng to a simmer and cook until potatoes and cauliflower are tender.

From: **Traveler's Club
and Tuba Museum**
2138 Hamilton Street
Okemos, Michigan

Cream of Morel Soup

1 pound morels, cleaned
3½ ounces butter
¾ cup diced wild leeks
⅔ cup flour
½ cup white wine
salt, pepper, thyme to taste
2 quarts plus ¾ cup
    chicken stock
1¼ cups heavy cream

Melt the butter. Add the morels and the leeks, cook for 10 minutes.

Add the flour and mix well. Cook over a low heat for 10 minutes. Add the wine and seasonings. Bring to a simmer. Add the chicken stock, stirring well and constantly to dissolve the roux of flour and butter. Bring to boil and simmer for ½ hour.

Add the cream and re-boil. Skim off any fat and serve.

From: **The Holly Hotel**
110 Battle Alley
Holly, Michigan

Danish Havarti Cheese Soup
with Fresh Dill and Potatoes

2 medium potatoes, diced
1 cup water
1½ tablespoons chicken base
3 cups milk
2 cups heavy cream
3 tablespoons butter or
  margarine
½ cup finely chopped onion
¼ cup finely chopped celery
3 tablespoons flour
2 tablespoons fresh dill,
  finely minced
½ teaspoon white pepper
½ pound Havarti cheese, cut
  into small cubes

In a small saucepan, with enough water to cover, cook potatoes until tender. Drain and set aside.

In a 2½-3 quart stockpot, add water, chicken base, milk and heavy cream. Bring to the boiling point, but do not boil.

Meanwhile, in a small pan, melt the butter and saute onion and celery until very soft and tender, approximately 5-7 minutes. When vegetables are soft, add flour and stir together so that the flour is absorbed. Continue to stir the roux for 1-1½ minutes, making certain not to let the flour brown. Turn off the heat and set aside.

Add the dill, white pepper and cheese to the very hot milk mixture. Stir constantly until cheese is completely melted and absorbed. Now add the vegetable roux and cook until thickened, stirring fairly constantly. This should take approximately 8-10 minutes.

Remove soup from heat and puree in blender until smooth. Add cooked potatoes to soup and garnish with tiny, buttered homemade croutons.

From: **The Hearthstone**
3550 Glade (Corner House Motel)
Muskegon, Michigan

Dill Pickle Soup
(Zupa Ogorkowa)

3 cups meat stock
2 cups potatoes, cubed
⅔ cup dill pickle liquid
4 large dill pickles, grated
1 cup mashed potatoes
1 tablespoon margarine
1 cup sour cream
salt and pepper to taste

Bring the meat stock, pickle liquid and cubed potatoes to a boil. Cook until potatoes are tender. Mix in margarine, grated pickles, add the mashed potatoes. Add salt and pepper to taste, stirring to smooth consistency. Add sour cream just before serving. Yield: 6 servings.

From: **Polish Village Cafe**
2990 Yeamans, east of Jos Campau
Hamtramck, Michigan

Gazpacho Blanco

2 large cucumbers, peeled
  and seeded
1 green pepper, skin removed
1 medium onion
1 clove garlic
2 egg yolks
¼ cup herb flavored vinegar
½ cup olive oil
1 scant teaspoon sugar
1 cup chicken stock
1 cup tomato juice
parsley, finely chopped
freshly cracked black pepper
dill weed, finely chopped
few thyme leaves
salt to taste

In a food processor, chop the cucumbers, pepper, onion and garlic. Add the egg yolks and herb flavored vinegar, then add the olive oil and the sugar. Finally, add the chicken stock and tomato juice.

Add the parsley, dill weed, pepper, thyme for taste and color. Serve the soup in a deep bowl surrounded by ice and offer the traditional vegetables on the side. The vegetables usually served in or with a gazpacho include tomatoes, green pepper, cucumber, and scallions.

From: **Restaurant Duglass**
29269 Southfield Road
Southfield, Michigan

Mediterranean Vegetable Soup

2 cups onion, cut in
½" chunks
¼ cup olive oil
1 pound sweet Italian sausage,
casing removed
½ cup ham cubed
1 tablespoon garlic, minced
2 bay leaves
1 (1 pound) can garbanzo
beans with juice
½ cup cubed carrots
1 sweet red pepper,
seeded and cubed
¼ cup celery leaves,
freshly chopped
4 dashes cayenne
1 teaspoon dried rosemary
or 1 tablespoon fresh
1 teaspoon dried basil
or 2 tablespoons fresh
1 cup cabbage, cubed
½ teaspoon black pepper
3 cups canned tomatoes
with juice
8 cups chicken broth

Gently saute the onions in the olive oil until soft and golden. Crumble the sausage, which you have removed from its casing, into the onions and olive oil. Saute until just cooked through. Then add the remaining ingredients.

Simmer for 1 hour until all the vegetables are tender and the flavors have melded.

From: **Tosi's Restaurant**
4337 Ridge Road
Stevensville, Michigan

Hungarian Mushroom Soup

4 tablespoons butter
2 cups diced onion
2 pounds sliced mushrooms
¾ cup dry white wine
6 tablespoons butter
6 tablespoons flour
3 cups milk
3 cups sour cream
1½ teaspoons Hungarian
   paprika
1 teaspoon salt
1 teaspoon dill weed
½ teaspoon pepper

Saute the onions and mushrooms in the butter in a large saute pan until the onions are translucent.

Add the wine and cook until the alcohol has boiled off, about 3-4 minutes. Remove from the heat and set aside.

In a 3 quart saucepan, over low heat, blend the flour and butter into a roux, stirring constantly for 4 5 minutes. Add the milk, continue whisking, increase heat to medium. Cook until mixture thickens, whisking occasionally.

Whisk the mushroom/onion mixture into the milk mixture. Then add the sour cream and seasonings, simmer over low heat for 10 minutes or until flavors are blended. Yield: 8 cups.

From: **Seva Restaurant**
314 East Michigan Avenue
Ann Arbor, Michigan

Mussel and Corn Chowder

18 mussels
½ cup white wine
few parsley stems
15 peppercorns, bruised
½ sprig thyme
4 shallots, minced
1 clove garlic, crushed
3 ears of corn, kernels
   cut off, set aside
⅓ cup leeks, sliced
⅓ cup diced carrot
⅓ cup diced onion

Soak the mussels in cold water for 1 hour, drain and rinse in fresh water.

In a stainless steel saucepan, bring to boil the wine, parsley, shallots, garlic and herbs. Add mussels, cover tightly and, over high heat, steam just until mussels open. Remove from heat, drain juice and reserve. Allow mussels to cool, remove them from shells, beard them and cut in halves.

In a heavy saucepan, melt butter, add vegetables and saute until transparent; dust with flour, stir for 2 minutes, add chicken

3 tablespoons unsalted
  butter
2 tablespoons flour
1 cup chicken broth
mussel juice
salt and pepper to taste
1 cup heavy cream
2 tablespoons chives

broth and mussel juice, bring to a simmer and cook for 15 minutes. Remove from heat, place in a blender and purée. Put back on heat, add corn and bring to a boil; add cream and mussels, reheat. Sprinkle with chives before serving. Yield: 6 servings.

From: **The Golden Mushroom**
18100 West 10 Mile Road
Southfield, Michigan

Swiss Onion Soup

3 cups thinly sliced onions
1 garlic clove, minced
¾ teaspoon dry mustard
1½ teaspoons salt
5 tablespoons unsalted
  butter
2 cups chicken stock
  or water
3 tablespoons flour
1½ cups milk
½ teaspoon bottled
  horseradish
1 tablespoon dry sherry
1½ cups freshly grated
  Gruyere
½ teaspoon pepper
½ teaspoon soy sauce
3 drops Tabasco
¼ teaspoon Worcestershire

In a kettle, cook the onion and the garlic with the mustard and salt in 2 tablespoons of the butter over moderate heat, stirring for 10-12 minutes, or until the onion is softened.

Add the stock and simmer the mixture, covered, for 20 minutes.

In a saucepan, melt the remaining 3 tablespoons butter over moderate heat. Add the flour and cook the roux, whisking, for 3 minutes. Remove the pan from the heat, whisk in the milk, scalded, and simmer the mixture, whisking, for 7 minutes. Add the horseradish, the sherry and the Gruyere and combine the mixture well. Add the cheese mixture to the onion mixture, stir in the pepper, soy sauce, the Tabasco, and the Worcestershire sauce, and simmer soup, stirring, for 10 minutes. Yield: 4 servings.

From: **Leelanau Country Inn**
149 East Harbor Highway
Maple City, Michigan

Cathy's Potato Leek Soup

4 tablespoons unsalted butter
2 medium leeks, chopped
4 cups celery, including tops,
    chopped
6 cups potatoes, diced
1 teaspoon salt
½ teaspoon pepper
1-2 cups water
2 cups white very sharp
    cheddar, grated
2 tablespoons cream cheese
1 quart milk
1 pint half & half

Saute leeks and celery in butter in heavy soup pot.

When tender, add potatoes, salt, pepper and water. Cook on medium heat until potatoes are soft.

Add cheese, cream cheese, and half & half, lower heat and cover until cheese melts.

For a creamy soup, blend in the food processor or blender. Return to soup pot, add milk, correct seasonings. Warm on low heat or place in large double boiler. If chunky soup is desired, leeks, celery, and potatoes should be chopped finely and not put through the processor.

Garnish with dill/parsley and serve with old fashioned pumpernickel bread. Yield: 12 generous servings.

From: **Garden Cafe
Detroit Gallery of
Contemporary Crafts**
301 Fisher Building
Detroit Michigan

Red Bean Basil Soup

2 tablespoons butter
2 ounces diced onions
1 ounce carrot, peeled
  and chopped
1 ounce celery, chopped
10 ounces chicken stock
4 ounces dried red beans
4 ounces diced tomatoes
salt and pepper to taste
dash Tabasco
1 teaspoon dried basil

Melt the butter and saute the onions, carrots and celery until soft. Add chicken stock, beans, seasoning, and tomatoes. Simmer over low flame until beans are soft, approximately 30 minutes.

Puree through a strainer and serve. Yield: 4 servings.

From: **Darby's Restaurant**
45199 Cass Avenue
Utica, Michigan

Wild Rice Bisque

3 strips bacon, thick
½ cup wild rice
½ cup diced onion
½ cup diced carrot
½ cup diced celery
6 cups rich chicken stock
salt and pepper
1 teaspoon fresh thyme
1½ cups heavy cream
2 tablespoons butter,
  softened
2 tablespoons flour
2 tablespoons fresh parsley,
  minced

Using good hickory smoked bacon, saute until crisp, then add rice and vegetables and saute until vegetables are crisp tender. Stir in stock and fresh thyme. Bring to boil, reduce heat, then simmer covered till rice is barely tender, about 30 minutes. Stir in cream and heat through. Mix together the butter and flour and add to soup to thicken. Add parsley and season with salt and pepper. Yield: About 6 servings.

From: **Tapawingo**
9502 Lake Street
Ellsworth, Michigan

Smoked Lake Michigan Whitefish and New Potato Chowder with Fresh Lemon Thyme

1 pound bacon, diced
1 medium onion, diced
3 celery stalks, chopped
¼ pound butter
¾ cup flour
3 quarts fish stock
1 bay leaf
3 pounds smoked whitefish
1 large bunch lemon thyme
1 teaspoon garlic, chopped
2 pounds new potatoes
½ quart heavy cream
white pepper and salt to taste

Saute the bacon first, then add the onion and celery.

In a separate pan, melt the butter and stir in the flour, making a roux. Cook for 5 minutes on low heat. Add the roux to the bacon-onion mixture. Slowly add the fish stock, stirring constantly to prevent lumps from forming. Let simmer.

Take the meat of the whitefish off the bones, saving the head, bones and skin. Put these in cheesecloth and add to the simmering stock for about 30-40 minutes. This will bring out the smoked flavor. Add about ½ of the fish meat and save the rest for garnish.

Save about 10 sprigs of the thyme for garnish. Chop the rest and add with the garlic and a bay leaf to soup while it simmers.

Dice up and cook the new potatoes in a separate pot. Cool and add to the soup about 5 minutes before serving. At the same time, stir in the heavy cream, add salt and pepper to taste. Garnish with the remaining whitefish and sprigs of lemon thyme. Yield: 10 servings.

From: **Periwinkle's**
400 West Main Street
Brighton, Michigan

Meat and Poultry

Michigan's chefs take their meat and poultry seriously. In this chapter you will find most of the more standard fare usually offered in a chapter on meat and poultry. You will also find recipes in here for venison and pheasant—meat and poultry to be sure, but what a difference! There is even a recipe for muskrat as it is served in a restaurant in Michigan.

You will also find some wonderful new things to do with old favorites like pork roast and chicken. I think you will agree that the exercise of imagination has not exceeded good taste.

Michigan Cassoulet

⅓ pound Michigan navy beans
1 quart rich duck or
    chicken stock
1 cup onion, diced
2 cloves garlic, minced
1 ham hock
1 pound pork shoulder, diced
½ pound venison sausage,
    sliced
½ pound smoked turkey
½ pound morels, cleaned
½ cup tomato sauce
salt, pepper, thyme

Rinse and soak beans overnight. On the following day, drain the beans. In a large pot bring the stock to a simmer with the beans. Add to this the ham hock, garlic, and the onions. Simmer this for about 1 hour. Drain the beans and return the liquid to the stove and reduce to about a cup.

Preheat oven to 350 degrees. Meanwhile, saute the pork and venison sausage till the meat is brown and the fat is rendered. Drain the excess fat from the pan. Now add to the pan the reduced stock, tomato sauce, beans, the meats, (also include the meat from the ham hock). Add the rest of the ingredients. Season with salt and pepper and thyme and simmer for about 15 minutes. Layer the mixture into individual casseroles and sprinkle the tops with buttered bread crumbs. Bake in the oven for about an hour.

From: **The Rowe Inn**
County Road C48
Ellsworth, Michigan

Zel-Zel Wot
(Beef Stewed in Red Pepper Sauce)

2 cups onions, finely chopped
½ cup spiced butter*
2 teaspoons garlic, finely
   chopped
1 teaspoon ginger root,
   finely chopped
¼ teaspoon fenugreek seed,
   ground
⅛ teaspoon ground cloves
⅛ teaspoon allspice
⅛ teaspoon nutmeg, freshly
   grated
freshly grated black pepper
¼ cup paprika
2 tablespoons berbere*
⅔ cup dry red wine
½ cup water
1 tomato, chopped
   and pureed
2 teaspoons salt
3 pounds lean, boned beef,
   cut in 2" chunks

*See recipes for spiced butter and berbere in Sauces & Seasonings section.

In a heavy 4-5-quart enameled casserole, cook the onions over a moderate heat for 5-6 minutes, until they are soft and dry. Slide the casserole back and forth over the heat, and stir the onions constantly to prevent burning. If necessary, remove the casserole from the heat occasionally to let it cool for a few moments. Stir in the spiced butter, and, when it begins to sputter, add the garlic, ginger, fenugreek, cloves, allspice and nutmeg, stirring well after each addition. Add the paprika and berbere, and stir over a low heat for 2-3 minutes. Stir in the wine, water, pureed tomato and salt, and bring the liquid to a boil.

Add the beef chunks and turn them about until they are evenly coated with sauce. Then reduce the heat to low, and cover partially. Simmer for about 1½ hours, or until the meat shows no resistance when pierced with the point of a small knife. Sprinkle the wot with a few grindings of pepper, and season to taste.

To serve, transfer the contents of the casserole to a deep, heated bowl or platter. Zel-zel wot, like doro wot, is traditionally served with injera, but it may also be served with Arab-style flat bread or boiled rice.

From:

The Blue Nile
Trappers Alley
508 Monroe Street
Detroit, Michigan

Mesquite Grilled Rack of Lamb
with Tomato Leek Basil Vinaigrette

Marinade for Rack of Lamb:
½ cup basil, packed, chopped
1 teaspoon garlic, chopped
¼ cup dry red wine
1 quart vegetable oil
1 tablespoon cracked
* black pepper*
¼ cup basil vinegar

**Tomato Leek
Basil Vinaigrette:**
2 leeks, white part sliced
4 tomatoes, peeled, seeded
* and julienned*
1 bunch basil, chopped
½ cup basil vinegar
¼ cup dry red wine
1 clove garlic, minced
¼ pound butter

Mix together ingredients for marinade and marinate rack of lamb for at least 6-8 hours.

Light the grill, using special mesquite charcoal or wood. Brush off any excess marinade, place lamb on grill and cook until medium rare, rotating so it doesn't burn. Serve with vinaigrette and buttered noodles tossed with chopped fresh rosemary .

Saute sliced leeks in a little olive oil, then add julienned tomatoes, chopped basil, basil vinegar, garlic and wine. Let reduce by ¼-½, then whip in butter in chunks to thicken. Pour on serving plate, put grilled lamb on top and serve with the buttered noodles tossed with chopped fresh rosemary.

From: **Periwinkle's**
400 West Main Street
Brighton, Michigan

Muskrat Saute

This dish is a specialty of Kola's Kitchen and was featured on National Public Radio's "All Things Considered."

1 muskrat (1 muskrat feeds
   1 person)
lots of water
1 cup salt
more water
bay leaves
1 large can stewed tomatoes
1 can tomato juice
1 large onion skin
1 clove garlic butter
soy sauce
2 ounces Liebfraumilch wine
½ garlic clove

To prepare muskrat, begin by skinning, removing all visible fat with your thumb and a paring knife. Open up the hind legs along the thighs from the base of tail to knee. Spot the musk sacks and remove.

Put 2-3 gallons of water in a pot. Add 1 cup of salt. Drop muskrat in. Bring to a boil. When water boils remove muskrat. Put another 2-3 gallons of cold water in pot. Dip muskrat, remove. Rub away excess fat and blood particles with thumbs. Redip.

Put 2-3 gallons of water in pot. Add ½ dozen bay leaves. Bring to a boil. Submerge muskrat. When water comes to second boil, remove the muskrat.

In another pot, put a couple of quarts of water, the tomatoes, juice, onion skin, and garlic. Bring to a boil. Put in muskrat and boil. When legs connected to the spine on the backside crack, the muskrat is done. You can also pinch meat for doneness, tenderness as you would with chicken.

Strain the sauce from the last boiling. Pour some into a pan, heat to the boiling point. Add flour to thicken for gravy. Set aside, keep warm.

Heat saute pan, add some soy sauce and 2-3 tablespoons butter. Put muskrat in pan, add the garlic and Liebfraumilch. Brown the muskrat on both sides. When browned, serve with mashed potatoes and sauerkraut, and gravy.

From: **Kola's Kitchen**
4500 13th Street
Wyandotte, Michigan

Almendrado

3½ pounds pork, trimmed,
   cut in 1" cubes
1 teaspoon salt
½ teaspoon pepper
3 garlic cloves, chopped
6 tablespoons peanut butter
1 medium onion, chopped
2 tablespoons vegetable oil
3 slices bread, crumbled
1 (12-ounce) can tomato sauce

Trim all fat from the pork and cut into cubes. Heat the pork in a heavy-bottomed saucepan with enough water to cover. Bring to a boil, reduce heat and simmer until pork is tender. about 40-45 minutes. Remove pork and set aside.

Skim fat from broth, if necessary, continue cooking until the broth is reduced to about 1 cup.

Heat the oil in a skillet. Add peanut butter and cook stirring, until peanut butter begins to turn golden brown. Peanut butter burns quickly so watch it carefully. Add the other ingredients together, except the pork, stirring well to mix thoroughly. Then add pork, bring to a simmer and let cook a few minutes.

From: **La Fuenta de Elena**
3456 West Vernor
Detroit, Michigan

Center Cut Cashew Pork

6 16-ounce pork chops
2 large carrots, diced
2 ribs celery, diced
1 Spanish onion, diced
¼ pound bacon, diced
½ cup cashews, toasted
    and minced
1 tablespoon tarragon
2 cups salad croutons
1 cup hot chicken broth
seasoning salt
paprika
½ cup pineapple juice

Blackberry Brandy Sauce:
1 small jar blackberry preserves
¼ cup blackberry brandy
1 tablespoon cornstarch

Slit pork chops or have your butcher do it. Place chops in roasting pan. Preheat oven to 300 degrees.

Saute carrots, celery, onion, bacon, tarragon and cashews in small amount of butter. When tender, toss in croutons and add hot chicken broth. Stuff mixture into pork chops, sprinkle with seasoning salt and paprika. Add pineapple juice to roasting pan for moisture, cover with foil and bake until 160 degrees on meat thermometer is or about 2 hours. Serve with a fruit sauce—example follows. Yield: 6 servings.

Put preserves and brandy in small, heavy-bottomed saucepan over low heat. Add cornstarch and cook until thickened.

From: **The Bay Pointe
Restaurant**
11456 Marsh Road
Shelbyville, Michigan

Roast Loin of Pork
with Apples and Yams

1 pork loin, 4-6 pounds
salt, pepper and sage

Apple Yam Mixture:
1 pound fresh yams, peeled
*   and diced*
8 ounces Granny Smith apples,
*   peeled and finely diced*
8 ounces celery, finely diced
4 ounces Spanish onion,
*   finely diced*
2 ounces fresh parsley, chopped
¼ teaspoon garlic
1 teaspoon fresh sage
6 tablespoons butter
6 tablespoons olive oil

Sauce:
1 ounce minced shallots
4 ounces (½ cup) white wine
1 quart veal demi-glace*
4 ounces concentrated
*   apple juice*
olive oil
butter

*demi-glace is simply meat stock
that has been boiled to reduce it
to a thick consistency.

Preheat oven to 350 degrees. Rub the pork roast with salt, pepper and the sage. Place in baking pan and roast in oven until roast is cooked as desired. A pork roast should cook 25-35 minutes a pound. Roast should be removed from the oven and allowed to rest 10-15 minutes before carving.

Saute all of the apple/yam mixture ingredients in 3 tablespoons each of the olive oil and butter. Add more if necessary. Continue sauteing until the ingredients are tender. Stir to cook evenly and prevent sticking.

Saute the shallots in a little of the oil and butter. Add the white wine and reduce until dry. Add the demi-glace and apple juice concentrate. Season to taste with salt and white pepper.

Slice tenderloin on the bias, arrange on divided bed of cooked wild rice and the apple/yam mixture. Ladle sauce over the pork and garnish with fresh steamed broccoli.

From: **Richard and Reiss**
273 Pierce Street
Birmingham, Michigan

Rabbit Pie with Sauteed Loin
White Wine, Tomato and Basil Sauce

4 young rabbits, boned,
  all meat removed
(36 ounces total),
  loins set aside
12 ounces pork fat back
4 eggs
2 small zucchini, julienned
½ pound mushrooms, sliced
2 small carrots, sliced thin
1 teaspoon minced garlic
1 tablespoon minced shallots
½ cup sundried tomatoes,
  julienned
¼ cup chopped fresh basil
2 tablespoons salt
1 tablespoon black pepper

Pastry dough:
3½ cups flour
½ pound butter
3 egg yolks
½ cup ice water

Grind rabbit and fatback in food processor on medium, chill for 1½ hours. Grind again, on fine, add eggs and mix well. Chill for 1 hour.

Saute zucchini, mushrooms, carrots, garlic and shallots in whole butter for 2 minutes. Squeeze dry and cool down.

Mix together the rabbit mixture, vegetables, tomatoes, basil, salt and pepper.

Preheat oven to 400 degrees. Make pastry dough: mix flour and butter together by hand until well incorporated. Add the egg yolks and water and mix until a smooth dough is formed. Roll some of the dough out to ¼" thickness and place in 9" springform pan with the dough coming to the top of the pan. Pack rabbit mixture into pan.

Using an egg wash made from 1 egg beaten with a few drops of water, eggwash the dough at the top of the pan. Roll out a 9½" circle of dough and place on top of rabbit mixture and seal well. Cut a ½" hole in the top crust to serve as a vent.

Bake until an internal temperature of 140 degrees is reached. Cool overnight in the refrigerator.

For the sauce, put the rabbit bones in a 400-degree oven and roast until they are brown. Place in a stock pot with onions, carrots, celery, thyme and bay leaf. Cover with water and simmer for 8 hours. Strain and reduce to 2 cups.

Sauce:

½ cup white wine
½ cup crushed tomatoes
1 tablespoon minced shallots
½ cup heavy cream
2 cups rabbit glace
½ cup chopped fresh basil
2 tablespoons butter
salt & pepper

Reduce white wine by ½. Add tomatoes, shallots, cream and glace. Bring to a boil, add basil, butter, salt and pepper to taste.

Preheat oven to 400 degrees. To serve, unmold the rabbit pie and cut into 8 equal pieces. Heat in oven for 10 minutes. Saute the reserved loins in smoking, clarified butter for 3 minutes on each side, remove and slice.

Heat sauce to a boil, spoon equal amounts of sauce on eight 10" plates. Place a wedge of pie on sauce and place 1 sliced loin on each plate. Yield: 8 servings.

From: **Cafe le Chat**
17001 Kercheval
Grosse Pointe, Michigan

Veal Nouvelle Cuisine

10 ounces veal, pounded
    thin
4 ounces artichokes, sliced
1 clove shallots, minced
salt and freshly cracked
    pepper
4 ounces clarified butter
6 ounces heavy cream
1 ounce vermouth
flour to dust

Dust veal with flour, season lightly with salt and pepper. Melt butter in saute pan. Brown veal in butter and turn over. Add minced shallots and artichokes to butter. When veal is done, remove veal and artichokes to warm plate.

Deglaze pan with vermouth. Add cream and reduce. Pour sauce over veal and adjust seasoning with salt and pepper. Yield: 1 serving.

From: **Oakley's
at the Haymarket**
161 East Michigan Avenue
Kalamazoo, Michigan

Scallopini alla Pasquale
(Veal with Sun-Dried Tomatoes)

2 pounds veal, cut
   and pounded into scallopine
flour
peanut oil
25-30 sun-dried tomato halves
25-30 fresh whole basil leaves
1-1½ pounds fontina cheese
non-stick cooking spray

Flour the veal and saute a few pieces at a time in hot peanut oil for just a few seconds on a side. Don't fully cook the veal at this point. Blot veal with paper towels to remove excess oil.

Preheat oven to 450 degrees. Arrange veal in a single layer on a baking tray that has been sprayed with a non-stick cooking spray. Layer each scallopine with sun-dried tomatoes, then fresh basil leaves and finally sliced fontina. Place in hot oven until cheese is well melted, about 10 minutes. Remove and serve. Garnish with red roasted peppers. Yield: 6-8 servings.

From: **Ristorante di Maria**
2080 Walnut Lake Road
West Bloomfield, Michigan

Braised Veal Shanks

2 veal shanks, cut in 8 pieces
   (have your butcher do this)
1 cup finely chopped onion
½ cup chopped carrot
½ cup chopped celery
¼ cup butter
1 teaspoon finely chopped garlic
½ cup flour
1 cup dry white wine
1½ cups beef stock

Saute onion, celery, carrot and garlic in butter until soft. Line the bottom of an 8-quart casserole dish with the soft vegetables.

Preheat oven to 350 degrees. Dip veal shanks in flour and saute in vegetable oil over medium-high heat until browned. Remove from saute pan and place in casserole on top of the vegetables. Skim fat from saute pan and deglaze with wine, boiling for

1½ cups chopped tomatoes
¼ cup thyme

3 minutes, pour over veal.

Using the same saute pan, add beef stock, thyme, chopped tomatoes, salt and pepper. Bring to a boil. Pour over veal until covered. Cover casserole and bake in oven for 2 hours. Remove veal from casserole, ladle sauce over veal and serve. Yield: 4 servings.

From: **Darby's Restaurant**
45199 Cass Avenue
Utica, Michigan

Venison Steaks with Mushrooms

4-8 vension steaks
salt and pepper
3 tablespoons clarified butter
1 tablespoon chopped shallot
* or 2 tablespoons chopped*
* green onion*
½ pound fresh mushrooms, sliced
⅓ cup madeira or dry sherry
⅓ cup heavy cream

Preheat large skillet or 2 medium ones. Season steaks with salt and pepper. Pour butter into skillet and add steaks immediately. Brown on one side and turn over. Cook to desired doneness, the same as you would beef. Transfer to platter, keep warm. Add shallots or green onions and mushrooms. Saute, stirring, until mushrooms turn gray. Add wine and continue cooking over high heat till most of the juice is evaporated. Add cream and cook down until it becomes a sauce. Yield: 4 servings.

From: **The Golden Mushroom**
18100 West Ten Mile Road
Southfield, Michigan

Boneless Chicken with Veal Forcemeat
in Champagne Sauce

2½-3 pound frying chicken
4 ounces ground veal
  (forcemeat)
½ ounce brandy
1 ounce heavy cream
1 egg
½ cup fresh bread crumbs
2 tablespoons fresh parsley,
  chopped

Champagne sauce:
1 shallot, minced
1 cup dry Champagne
1 cup chicken stock
¼ cup sliced mushrooms

Bone chicken in a manner that gives you two half chickens with wing bone remaining. Mix the veal with the brandy, cream, egg, bread crumbs and parsley.

Preheat oven to 350 degrees. Use the cavity created to place the veal forcemeat to form a dome shape with the wing bone standing upright. Wrap the chicken with a 2″ strip of parchment paper to hold its shape. Baste with butter, salt and pepper. Bake for 20 minutes, then remove paper and return to oven until cooked.

Saute shallots in a little butter until soft. Add champagne, reduce by ¾. Add chicken stock, reduce by ½. Add mushrooms, thicken with a bit of cornstarch, add salt and pepper to taste. Serve over chicken.

From: **Arie's Cafe**
127 East Bridge Street
Plainwell, Michigan

Chicken Dijon

8 3-ounce boneless chicken
   breasts—skinned, trimmed,
   carefully pounded flat
8 16/20-count shrimp, cooked,
   peeled and deveined
8 tablespoons unsalted butter
12 fresh mushrooms, minced
1 tablespoon minced shallots
1 teaspoon minced garlic
¾ cup pale dry sherry
1½ pints heavy cream
2-3 tablespoons Dijon mustard

Melt half the butter in a heavy skillet over medium heat. Dredge the chicken in the flour and lightly saute until done. Remove chicken from the pan. Add remaining butter over medium heat and saute mushrooms, shallot and garlic until almost dry. Add sherry and reduce until almost dry. Add the heavy cream and reduce until thick. Add mustard and season to taste. Return chicken to sauce with the shrimp and heat slowly until all is heated through. Serve 2 pieces chicken per person with a shrimp atop each piece. Ladle sauce over all. Fresh pasta is a great accompaniment. Yield: 4 servings.

From: **Stafford's
          Bay View Inn**
          Petosky, Michigan

Doro Wot
(Chicken in Red Pepper Sauce)

2½-3 pound chicken,
  cut into 8 serving pieces
2 tablespoons lemon juice
2 teaspoons salt
2 cups finely chopped onion
⅓ cup spiced butter*
1 tablespoon scraped fresh
  ginger root, finely chopped
1 tablespoon chopped garlic
¼ teaspoon ground cardamom
⅛ teaspoon nutmeg,
  preferably freshly grated
¼ cup berbere*
2 tablespoons paprika
¼ cup dry white or red wine
¾ cup water
4 hard-boiled eggs,
  peeled
freshly ground black pepper

*The recipes for niter k'ibe (spiced butter) and berbere are in the Sauces and Seasonings chapter.

Pat the chicken dry with paper towels and rub pieces with lemon juice and salt. Let the chicken rest at room temperature for 30 minutes.

In an ungreased, heavy 3-4 quart enamelled casserole, cook the onions over moderate heat for 5-6 minutes or until they are soft and dry. Shake the pan and stir constantly to prevent the onions from burning; if necessary reduce the heat or lift the pan occasionally from the stove to let it cool for a few minutes before returning it to the heat. Stir in the spiced butter, and, when it begins to sputter, add the garlic, ginger, cardamom and nutmeg, stirring well after each addition. Add the berbere and paprika, and stir over a low heat for 2-3 minutes. Then pour in the wine and water and, still stirring, bring to a boil over high heat. Cook briskly, uncovered for about 5 minutes, or until the liquid in the pan has reduced to the consistency of heavy cream.

Pat the chicken dry and drop it into the simmering sauce, turning the pieces about with a spoon until they are coated on all sides. Reduce the heat to the lowest point. Cover and simmer for 30 minutes or until the chicken is tender when pierced with the point of a knife. Sprinkle the stew with pepper, and season to taste. With the tines of a fork, pierce ¼" deep holes over the entire surface of each egg. Then put them in the sauce and turn them about.

To serve, turn the entire contents of the

casserole into a deep, heated platter or bowl. Doro wot is traditionally eaten with injera, but may also be served with Arab-style flat bread or hot, boiled rice. Plain yogurt in separate bowls may be served with the wot.

From: **The Blue Nile**
Trappers Alley
508 Monroe Street
Detroit, Michigan

Pollo Gordinicina

6 boneless chicken breasts
¼ cup cream sherry
⅛ cup sweet vermouth
13 ounces butter
1 cup sliced mushrooms
¼ cup chopped proscuitto
¼ cup boiled onions
¼ teaspoon parsley

Lightly saute the chicken breasts in oil. Set aside and keep warm.

Add all the other ingredients together in a heavy bottom saucepan over medium heat, stirring to prevent burning. Stir until the sauce looks nice and creamy. Add the chicken and bring sauce to a boil. Simmer gently until sauce reaches desired thickness. Yield: 6 servings.

From: **Antonio's Restaurant**
20311 Mack Avenue
Grosse Pointe Woods, Michigan

Chicken Stew in Beggar's Purses

To stew chicken:
1 whole chicken
4 ribs celery, cut roughly
3 carrots, peeled,
  cut roughly
2 small onions, diced
bouquet garni (thyme, oregano
  and bay leaf)
1½ gallons water

½ pound button mushrooms
2 leeks, cleaned and diced
  (the green part of the leek to
  be blanched for 10 seconds
  in boiling water and cut into
  julienne)
1 carrot, diced
2 ribs celery, diced
⅛ teaspoon minced garlic
1½ cups heavy cream
½ pound Gruyere cheese
6 large crepes

Note—for crepes, use your favorite recipe or "Mastering the Art of French Cooking" by Julia Child, Simone Beck and Louise Bertholle.

Also note that the amount of heavy cream may vary according to the amount of chicken broth you have left. Be sure the leeks are not blanched too much, or they will not tie properly.

Preheat oven to 350 degrees. Put all ingredients into pot with chicken and cook on medium heat until chicken meat comes off the bones easily. Remove the pot from the stove and allow the liquid and chicken to cool down. When cool, take the chicken out of liquid and take all meat off the bones and dice. Put liquid back on stove and reduce to ¼ of original quantity. This shoud have a good flavor to it and season it to taste. Strain and put aside.

In a saucepan, put 2 tablespoons butter and saute vegetables until partly cooked. Add chicken broth and allow to reduce until it takes on a thickened consistency. Add heavy cream and garlic and let cook for a few minutes. Add chicken and stir in thoroughly. Season to taste. Allow to cool down before finishing the dish. In center of crepe, spoon some chicken mixture, and add to this a small amount of grated cheese. Create a sack by bunching up the crepe and tie the green leek around the top as tightly as possible. This should give you a purse-like appearance. In ovenwear dish, place them in oven and allow to get hot prior to serving, about 15 minutes. Yield: 6 servings.

From: **Chez Raphael**
2700 Sheraton Drive
Novi, Michigan

Breast of Turkey
with Raspberries

12 small medallions
   of turkey breast meat
6 tablespoons butter
1 tablespoon shallots,
   chopped
3 ounce raspberry liqueur
1 ounce raspberry vinegar
handful of fresh
   raspberries
1 cup heavy cream

Slightly flatten the turkey medallions and saute in the butter. Remove from pan and keep warm. Add the shallots and saute lightly. Add the raspberry liqueur and raspberry vinegar and reduce by $2/3$. Add the raspberries. Then add the heavy cream and reduce the mixture until it coats a spoon.

Place turkey medallions on plates and spoon sauce over them. Garnish with fresh raspberries. Yield: 6 servings. Chicken may be substituted for turkey.

From: **The Clarkston Cafe**
18 South Main Street
Clarkston, Michigan

Grilled Michigan Pheasant Legs
with Traverse City Dried Cherries

These grilled pheasant legs are often offered at luncheon. They are boned out and all the fine cartilege in lower leg is removed. Usually two per order are served.

12 pheasant legs, boned
1½ cups port wine
1 apple, chopped
1 onion, chopped
1 orange, sliced, peeled
¼ cup olive oil
1 bay leaf
2 cups rich chicken stock
1 cup julienne leeks
½ cup dried cherries,
    chopped
4 tablespoons butter

Put pheasant legs in marinade made from the wine, apple, onion, orange, olive oil and bay leaf. Marinate for 24 hours.

Remove legs from marinade. Reduce the marinade by ⅔. Strain out spice, apple, onion, orange. Add the chicken stock and reduce to 1½ cups. Add leeks and cherries.

Grill the pheasant legs until done. Reheat the sauce and stir in the butter. Pour sauce on plate and put legs on sauce. Yield: 6 servings.

From: **The Money Tree**
333 West Fort
and Washington Boulevard
Detroit, Michigan

Fish & Seafood

Fish and Seafood

Chefs in Michigan have responded to the availability of fresh seafood with enthusiasm. Included in this chapter are many tantalizing recipes for new ways to treat fish and seafood. There are also recipes that deal with locally produced fare, like smoked whitefish, offering new ways to fix old favorites.

The popularity of fish and seafood is still climbing as people discover that it is not only good for you, but it tastes wonderful. There are lots of ways to fix what anyone among your family and friends catch. Get out the saute pans, the white wine and enjoy!

Fettucine alla Maria

¾ cup unsalted butter
3 cups heavy cream
¼ cup toasted bread crumbs
pinch white pepper
4 teaspoons minced
    green onions
½ teaspoon garlic, minced
¼ cup dry white wine
12 jumbo shrimp
4 4-ounce lobster tails
12 artichoke hearts
1 cup Pecorino Romano cheese,
    freshly grated

Combine the butter, garlic, wine, bread crumbs, cream, green onions and white pepper in a 14″ saute pan. Place over a high heat, mashing butter to blend until smooth. Bring to a boil, stirring frequently and turn heat to low.

Cut the lobster tails into 8 pieces each, peel and devein the shrimp and halve the artichoke hearts. Add to the sauce and saute until sauce is thickened and seafood is cooked, approximately 5 minutes.

Add the freshly grated Romano cheese, turn heat back to high to melt the cheese fast, stirring constantly, about 30 seconds.

Serve over hot fettucine cooked al dente. Yield: 4 servings.

From: **Ristorante di Maria**
          2080 Walnut Lake Road
          West Bloomfield, Michigan

Poached Halibut
in Cucumber Sauce

6 5-6 ounce halibut fillets
1 cup cold water
Pesto*
½ bottle dry white wine
4-5 shallots, chopped
crushed black pepper

Pesto:
2 cups fresh basil, packed
2 cloves fresh garlic
¼ cup pine nuts
½ cup olive oil
¼ cup Parmesan cheese,
   freshly grated
1-2 tablespoons Romano,
   freshly grated

Cucumber Sauce:
2 potatoes, scrubbed but
   not peeled
1 small onion
salt
juice of ½ lemon
1 tablespoon vinegar
2 cucumbers, peeled
1 cup sour cream
½ cup fish stock from
   cooking halibut
sprigs of fennel and dill

To make the pesto, put the basil, pine nuts, cheese and garlic in a blender or food processor, slowly adding the olive oil until well blended. Pesto may be frozen successfully.

Preheat oven to 350 degrees. Set fillets in a buttered pan that has been sprinkled with the chopped shallots. Spread the pesto on the fish. Add the water, wine and crushed black pepper. Set in the oven and bake for about 15 minutes. Do not overcook. Fish is properly cooked when the flesh is opaque and flakes easily when touched with a fork. Cool and strain off the stock.

For the cucumber sauce, cook the potatoes and onion until soft, put in a food processor or blender with some liquid and blend until smooth like a soft malt. Add to the seasoned cucumbers and then add the fish stock, which you have reserved from cooking the halibut. Add the sour cream and season. Some fresh dill and fennel sprigs should be added for additional flavor. Test for salt and pepper. Put fish on a serving platter, pour sauce over, garnish with sprigs of the fresh herbs. Serve with a chilled dry white wine. Yield: 6 servings.

From: **Restaurant Duglass**
29269 Southfield
Southfield, Michigan

Linguine Pesce

1 teaspoon diced garlic

1 ounce peanut oil

¼ cup white onions,
   diced and blanched

1 teaspoon Italian
   parsley, fresh

¼ cup unsalted butter

¼ cup dry white wine

1 teaspoon fresh basil

8 littleneck clams

8 slices green pepper,
   ¼" wide

16 mussels, scrubbed
   thoroughly

8 large mushrooms,
   sliced thinly

8 jumbo shrimp, peeled &
   deveined

2 cups marinara sauce*

1 pound bay scallops

*A good, standard marinara
sauce may be found in "The Joy of
Cooking."

Saute the garlic in the oil over high heat until lightly browned. Add parsley, basil, peppers, mushrooms, onions, butter, white wine. Open clams over the pan to catch the juices, being careful not to break any shells into the pan. Set the clams aside in their shells.

Reduce the sauce slightly over high heat, then add marinara sauce and bring to a boil. Add clams, mussels, and shrimp. Saute these over medium heat until the mussels open. Add the scallops and saute for approximately 3 minutes longer. Serve over hot linguine al dente. Yield: 4 servings.

From: **Ristorante di Maria**
2080 Walnut Lake Drive
West Bloomfield, Michigan

Pickerel in Phyllo

4 pickerel fillets
4 cups chicken stock
1 cup Chablis
2 celery stalks, minced
2 carrots, minced
1 onion, minced
6 sprigs parsley
salt & pepper to taste
6 tablespoons butter
3 tablespoons flour
8 sheets phyllo dough

Preheat oven to 350 degrees. Place pickerel fillets in baking pan, add stock, wine, vegetables, salt and pepper. Cover with foil and bake until fish is barely cooked, approximately 15 minutes.

Remove and cool pickerel fillets. Reduce stock to about 2 cups. Make a roux by blending 3 tablespoons flour with 3 tablespoons of the butter in a saucepan and cooking over medium heat. Cook for 2 minutes, stirring constantly. Add reduced stock to roux, bring to a boil, stirring constantly until mixture has thickened.

Preheat oven to 375 degrees. Brush sheet of phyllo with melted butter and top with another sheet of phyllo and again brush with butter. Lay one pickerel fillet crosswise to length of phyllo. Top with 1 tablespoon of sauce. Fold sides of phyllo inward to partially cover the fillet. Roll fillet in phyllo the entire length of the sheet. Brush with butter. Repeat with remaining pickerel fillets. Place on baking sheet and bake until phyllo is nicely browned, or about 15 minutes. We serve this topped with a hollandaise sauce. Yield: 4 servings.

From: **The Victorian Inn**
1229 Seventh Street
Port Huron, Michigan

Salmon Steaks au Poivre
with Lemon Caper Sauce

8 8-ounce salmon steaks
¼ cup vegetable oil
1 tablespoon crushed
   black pepper
¾ teaspoon granulated garlic
2 tablespoons clarified
   butter

Sauce:
¼ cup dry white wine
2 cups heavy cream
2 lemons, juiced
salt and white pepper to taste
pinch granulated garlic
2 tablespoons capers
   (nonparelles)

Rub salmon steaks with the vegetable oil and press the pepper into the steaks. Sprinkle on the garlic.

Preheat oven to 250 degrees. In a heavy saute pan over medium heat, add the clarified butter. When butter is quite hot—but not smoking—saute the steaks 2 minutes on each side. Remove the steaks from the pan and put in the oven to keep warm. Pour off any excess butter and oil.

Deglaze the pan with the white wine. Reduce by ⅔. Add the cream, lemon juice, salt, pepper and garlic. Reduce the cream over medium heat until it achieves a sauce like consistency. Add the capers and reduce the cream a little further.

Remove the steaks from the oven and place on a serving platter. Top each steak with an equal portion of the caper sauce. Garnish with parsley. Yield: 4 servings.

From: **South Street
Culinary Shoppe**
116 West South Street
Kalamazoo, Michigan

Scallops Shamay

¼ cup butter (½ stick)
36 large sea scallops
36 large mushrooms (1 pound)
1 can artichoke hearts
⅓ cup butter
½ cup flour
½ teaspoon salt
¼ teaspoon white pepper
1 cup chicken broth
1 cup dry white wine
1 cup half & half cream
3 cups Monterey Jack
    cheese, shredded
1 cup Romano, freshly
    grated
1½ cups bread crumbs
¼ cup butter, melted
paprika

Preheat oven to 350 degrees. Melt ¼ cup butter in large skillet over medium heat. Add scallops and saute just until opaque, about 1-2 minutes. Be careful not to overcook.

Using a slotted spoon, transfer scallops to six individual ramekins, (you may use an ovenproof casserole if you don't have ramekins), dividing evenly. Add mushrooms to same skillet and saute until tender. Divide among the ramekins, then divide the artichoke hearts, which you have drained, patted dry and quartered.

Then melt the ⅓ cup butter in the same skillet over low heat and whisk in flour. Simmer for 2 minutes, stirring constantly. Do not allow roux to brown. Gradually whisk in broth, wine, and half & half, letting the sauce thicken before adding the next liquid. Simmer until thickened. Add cheeses one cup at a time, stirring constantly until melted. Season sauce to taste with salt and pepper. Ladle sauce over ingredients in the ramekins, distributing evenly to cover.

Combine the bread crumbs with the melted butter in a medium bowl to blend thoroughly. Sprinkle evenly over ramekins or casserole. Dust with paprika. Bake until crumbs are golden and sauce is bubbling, about 15 minutes. Serve hot. Yield: 6 servings.

From: **Grande Mere Inn**
5880 Red Arrow Highway
Stevensville, Michigan

Steamed Scallops with Garlic Escarole

2 pounds bay scallops
½ teaspoon salt
1 tablespoon minced garlic
4 tablespoons extra
   virgin olive oil
10 cups loosely packed
   escarole or romaine
½ teaspoon red pepper flakes
½ cup sun-dried tomatoes

Sauce:
¾ cup extra virgin olive oil
1 teaspoon lime zest
2 tablespoons fresh lime juice
½ teaspoon freshly
   ground black pepper

To make the sauce, simply combine all the ingredients, beating thoroughly to emulsify and heat to warm. Keep warm.

Place scallops in steamer, sprinkle with salt. Cook till barely done, remove from heat. (Scallops are done when they become opaque.) Keep warm.

Heat the olive oil until very hot, add the garlic and pepper flakes. Cook about 20 seconds, then add escarole. Saute until tender, and toss in tomatoes.

Toss lightly and remove from heat, and place equal amounts on serving plates, making a nest on each plate for scallops.

Place scallops in nest on each plate and lightly cover with sauce. Garnish with lime section and serve with your choice of vegetable. Yield: 5 servings.

From:

**Thornapple
Village Inn**
455 Thornapple Village, SE
Ada, Michigan

Curried Shrimp

12 ounces good marmalade
2 tablespoons Dijon mustard
2 tablespoons horseradish
1 tablespoon curry powder

melted butter
1 clove garlic, minced
30 jumbo shrimp, peeled
  and deveined

In a heavy saucepan mix together the marmalade, mustard, horseradish and curry powder. Simmer approximately 10 minutes over low heat, stirring to prevent sticking.

In a saute pan, melt the butter, add the garlic and the shrimp. When shrimp are almost cooked—no more than 5-7 minutes, add the sauce and toss until all the shrimp are well coated. Serve immediately. Yield: 6 servings.

From: **Bay Pointe Restaurant**
11456 Marsh Road
Shelbyville, Michigan

Shrimp and Pesto Salad

50 shrimp
1 cup dry white wine
1 cup water
10-15 peppercorns
bay leaf or two

2 bunches green onions,
    chopped
2 red bell peppers
2 green peppers
1 cup ground hazelnuts
1½ cups freshly grated
    Parmesan cheese
10 ounces broccoli flowerets,
    blanched
10 ounces shell pasta

Pesto Vinaigrette:

1½ cups olive oil
3 tablespoons red wine
    vinegar
6 tablespoons garlic,
    minced
¾ cup fresh basil,
    chopped

In a heavy saucepan, put the shrimp with the wine, water, peppercorns and bay leaf. Bring just to a boil, put lid and remove from heat. Shrimp will cook in hot poaching liquid and not be overdone. When shrimp are done, remove shells and devein, reserving liquid for soup stock.

Roast the peppers. This is done by holding pepper on long cooking fork over a flame and turning gradually. The skin can then be easily removed. Peppers may also be roasted in the oven under the broiler, turning to expose all sides to broiler. Remove from oven, put in heavy brown paper bag and allow steam to help loosen skin. Remove skins and set aside.

Roast hazelnuts in a 350 degree oven whole, brushed with olive oil until brown, then grind in food processor or blender.

The broccoli should be blanched in boiling water and then plunged in cold water to refresh.

For the pesto put the basil and garlic in the blender and gradually add the olive oil in a steady stream.

Assemble all the ingredients of the pesto in a large bowl and toss with the pesto dressing. Yield: 10 servings.

From: **The Moveable Feast**
326 West Liberty Street
Ann Arbor, Michigan

Red Snapper with Avocado Lime Butter

4 ounces sauterne
3 ounces lime juice
2 shallots, peeled and minced
a bay leaf
1 tablespoon fresh tarragon,
  chopped
pinch fresh thyme
1 ripe avocado, peeled
  and diced finely
1 pound unsalted butter
1 teaspoon cracked
  black pepper
salt to taste
1 ounce each red, yellow,
  green bell peppers, diced
Red snapper or any firm
  fleshed fish

In an enamel or stainless steel saucepan, reduce wine, lime juice, shallots, bay leaf, tarragon, thyme until only about 2 ounces of liquid remains.

Put avocado in blender or food processor and add reduced mixture. Mix until blended thoroughly.

Add in softened bits of butter with cracked pepper and salt to taste. When thoroughly blended, fold in colored peppers and mix, just until distributed equally.

Roll the mixture in parchment paper, making a roll about 1-1½" in diameter. Freeze until ready to use.

Season any firm fleshed fish, such as red snapper or swordfish, with salt, pepper and oil. Grill just until center is opaque.

Before plating the fish, slice 2 or 3 thin medallions of avocado lime butter and place on fish. Hold under the broiler just until the medallions begin to melt and then transfer to a plate. Serve with seasonal vegetables and boiled red skin potatoes or garlic peppered linguine with chopped herbs.

From:

The Bay Cafe at Lumberton
1050 West Western Avenue
Muskegon, Michigan

Whitefish Grenoble Style

1 6-8 ounce whitefish fillet
milk
flour
salt
pepper
granulated garlic
clarified butter

Grenoble Sauce:
½ cup diced lemon
¼ cup diced tomato
¼ cup capers
1 ounce fresh butter

Mix the salt, pepper, and garlic with the flour. Coat the fillets with milk, then with the seasoned flour.

Heat saute pan, when hot add 1 ounce clarified butter. Place fillet in pan, skin side down. Cook until golden brown, turn over and cook until done.

Remove fillet onto a plate while pan is still hot, wipe the pan out with a clean damp rag. Place back on the stove. Add fresh butter; when it starts to brown add 1 tablespoon of the Grenoble, pour over the fillet and serve.

From:

Arie's Cafe
127 East Bridge Street
Plainwell, Michigan

Steamed Lake Superior Whitefish
with Ginger Chive Vinaigrette

1 tablespoon olive oil
6 5-6 ounce portions of
   whitefish, pinboned
1 tablespoon shallot, minced
salt and pepper to taste
1 cup dry white wine

2 tablespoons olive oil
2 cups allumette potatoes*
2 cups pea pods, blanched

*shoestring potatoes,
   deep fried, golden brown and
   crispy.

Ginger Chive Vinaigrette:
1 egg yolk
1 teaspoon Dijon mustard
2 tablespoons ginger, minced
1 teaspoon white pepper
1 teaspoon shallot, minced
2 teaspoons soy sauce
1 teaspoon garlic, minced
¾ ounce lemon juice
6 ounces olive oil

Preheat oven to 400 degrees. Lightly oil bottom of baking pan. Lay fish on bottom making sure that the fillets do not touch. Sprinkle with shallot, salt and pepper and pour wine all around. Cover with buttered parchment paper or buttered foil and bake for approximately 15 minutes or until done.

While fish is steaming, prepare allumette potatoes. Drain on paper towels. Heat 2 tablespoons of olive oil in saute pan. Quickly heat the pea pods in the oil. On warmed plates divide the ginger vinaigrette sauce (recipe follows), pea pods and potatoes. Scatter over the plate. Arrange the filets on top. Pop in the oven for 30 seconds to assure sauce is warm.

Make this sauce at least 8 hours in advance, 1 hour before service, put out to reach room temperature.

Blend the first 8 ingredients in a bowl. Slowly drizzle in the olive oil, beating thoroughly, being sure it emulsifies.

From: **The Money Tree**
333 West Fort &
Washington Boulevard
Detroit, Michigan

Vegetables

Vegetables

Michigan chefs seem to expand their creativity to every culinary corner, including vegetables. We've come a long way from the era of just throwing vegetables in a pot and boiling them to unrecognizability. Or even from the stage of taking them in little frozen rectangles and dropping them in boiling water.

Here are some wonderful ways to fix vegetables, so that no one need ever say again, "Do I have to eat this?" Some of these vegetable recipes are good enough to be eaten all by themselves—the ultimate test of taste.

Broccoli/Almond Saute

²/₃ cup olive oil
¹/₃ cup butter or margarine
1 tablespoon minced garlic
2 cups sliced almonds
2 teaspoons lemon juice
2 teaspoons rosemary
2½ cups dry white wine
2 teaspoons salt
6 cups broccoli, cut in flowerets

Parboil broccoli lightly. It should still be crunchy. Melt olive oil and butter over high heat until the mixture is foamy and almost smoking. Quickly stir in garlic and almonds. Stir and fry until they are browned (only a minute or two). Add lemon juice and rosemary. Remove from heat. Stir in wine and salt.

Pour oil and almond mixture over broccoli.

Toss with several shakes of freshly ground black pepper. Refrigerate until ready to serve, then lightly saute broccoli and almonds in hot fry pan until heated through and tender. (You will not need butter as the broccoli is already coated.)

While it is marinating, the broccoli will keep nicely in the refrigerator for several days.

From: **Traveler's Club and Tuba Museum**
22138 Hamilton Street
Okemos, Michigan

Sauteed Leeks and Carrots

4 cups of washed leeks,
    whites only
1 cup julienne carrots
4 tablespoons butter
one ounce dry white wine
salt and pepper

Julienne leeks and carrots, after peeling carrots and cleaning leeks. Saute in butter over a low flame until soft. Add white wine, salt and pepper. Saute briefly and serve. Yield: 4 servings.

From: **Darby's Restaurant**
45199 Cass Avenue
Utica, Michigan

Brandywine DeKalb Potatoes

6-8 medium to large potatoes
¼ cup soft butter
2 cups medium sharp grated
    cheddar cheese
2 cups sour cream
⅓ cup chopped onion
¼ teaspoon pepper
1 teaspoon salt

Parboil potatoes until tender, cool and grate coarsely.

Preheat oven to 325 degrees. Combine all above ingredients and place in 2 quart casserole dish. Top with small amount of additional melted butter. Bake for 45 minutes to one hour.

From: **Brandywine
Pub and Food**
2125 Horton Road
Jackson, Michigan

Potato Pancakes

4 cups grated raw potatoes
4 tablespoons flour
4 eggs
2 teaspoons salt
1 teaspoon pepper
¼ cup grated onion

Pour off some of the liquid from the grated potatoes. Add all other ingredients and mix thoroughly. Spoon mixture, as thinly as possible, onto a heated pan (make certain the pan has a generous amount of whatever cooking oil you prefer). Fry on both sides until golden brown. Yield: 4-6 servings.

From: **Polish Village Cafe**
2990 Yeamans,
east of Jos Campau
Hamtrack, Michigan

New Potatoes in Sour Cream

2 pounds small red potatoes
1 cup sour cream
3 tablespoons fresh parsley
6 green onions
1 tablespoon freshly grated
    black pepper
1 tablespoon seasoned salt

Boil the potatoes with skins on, until just fork tender. Drain and add sour cream and mix. Sprinkle with chopped fresh parsley and chopped green onions. Add pepper and seasoned salt.

Serve hot with your favorite meat or cool to take on a picnic. Great and easy!

From: **The Ample Pantry**
5629 Stadium Drive
Kalamazoo, Michigan

Peperonata Piccante

7 medium potatoes. sliced,
  then chopped into chunks
5 cayenne peppers,
  finely chopped
1 large onion, finely chopped
7 green peppers,
  cut in large chunks
3 cups fresh tomatoes,
  peeled and chopped
6 ounces olive oil

Saute potatoes, cayenne peppers and onions in olive oil for 10 minutes. Then add the green peppers and tomatoes and cook for another 15 minutes. Serve with a good, crusty bread.

May be served over bread for an openfaced sandwich. If you do not like hot foods, delete or reduce the cayenne peppers.

From: **Argiero's Restaurant**
300 Detroit Street
Ann Arbor, Michigan

Fresh Spinach Pasta

5 ounces flour
5 ounces semolina flour
2 eggs
1 egg yolk
1 tablespoon avocado oil
3 cloves garlic
½ cup chopped fresh spinach,
  packed

Cook spinach in boiling salted water. Shock under cold water, and squeeze dry to remove as much water as possible. Place spinach in food processor with garlic and oil and puree. Add the other ingredients, either kneading by hand or using a dough hook on an electric mixer. Knead or mix until smooth, adding more flour if necessary. Run through pasta rolling machine and cut into desired shape. Cook in boiling salted water for 1 minute. Drain, but do not shock. Instead pour pasta onto a cookie sheet and moisten with a small amount of avocado oil. Yield: 4 servings.

From: **Stafford's
Bay View Inn**
Petosky, Michigan

Sauteed Spinach

1 pound fresh spinach,
   washed well
2 tablespoons butter
4 tablespoons extra virgin
   olive oil
4 tablespoons chopped
   proscuitto
2 tablespoons minced garlic

Combine the olive oil and butter in a 12" skillet, heat until the butter melts, then saute the proscuitto and garlic until the garlic becomes tender. Add the fresh spinach and cook uncovered until the spinach is wilted and excess water has disappeared. Yield: 6 small servings.

From: **Tosi's**
4337 Ridge Road
Stevensville, Michigan

Kik Alit'cha

3 tablespoons chopped garlic
1 cup shallots, chopped
3 heaping tablespoons
   spiced butter*
1 heaping tablespoon ginger
   and garlic powder, mixed
3 cups split peas or lentils,
   cooked
1 teaspoon turmeric

*Recipe for spiced butter found in Sauces chapter.

Brown the garlic in a little water. Add the shallots and brown slightly. Add a ½ cup water and boil for 20 minutes or until the water has evaporated. Add the butter and continue to stir while it melts. Put in the garlic and ginger and stir until the powder is dissolved before adding the split peas or lentils. Then add the turmeric and salt to taste and serve hot with injera.

From: **The Blue Nile**
Trappers Alley
508 Monroe Street
Detroit, Michigan

Gratin of Squash and Zucchini

4 ounces butter
4 ounces olive oil
3 leeks, white part only,
   trimmed and cleaned
4 medium zucchini,
   peeled and grated
1 butternut squash,
   peeled and grated
cayenne, salt and pepper
   to taste
1 tablespoon tarragon
¾ cup freshly grated
   Parmesan cheese
3 medium zucchini,
   cut in ¼" slices

Melt butter and oil in saucepan. Add leeks and saute in pan. Remove from pan. Add grated zucchini and saute. Remove from pan. Add grated butternut squash, saute and remove. Reduce any liquid remaining in the saucepan to a syrup and pour over sauteed vegetables. Season with salt, pepper, cayenne and tarragon. Add Parmesan cheese.

Preheat oven to 400 degrees. Butter a casserole dish and arrange sliced zucchini alternating with the vegetable mixture. Sprinkle with Parmesan cheese and bake for 30 minutes.

From: **The Moveable Feast**
6 West Liberty Street
Ann Arbor, Michigan

Yam Puree

3-4 large yams
1 teaspoon grated orange zest
2 tablespoons butter
2 tablespoons lemon juice
salt, pepper
½ cup coarsely chopped walnuts

Bake yams at 350 degrees until soft. Split lengthwise, scoop out pulp, discard shells.

Place pulp in food processor, add rest of ingredients, except the walnuts, and puree. Remove and stir in walnuts. Serve warm. Yield: 6 servings.

From: **The Golden Mushroom**
18100 West Ten Mile Road
Southfield, Michigan

Salads &

Salad

Dressings

Salads and Salad Dressings

Salads are dishes that lend themselves well to experimentation. There seems almost no limit to what can be done with vegetables, fruits, lettuces and other leafy greens. The addition of meats, seafoods, and poultry extend the variety almost exponentially.

Accompanying these new combinations are new dressings. We have new vinegars, new to us at least. Dijon mustard has become such a staple that it is offered even in fast food chains; as a salad dressing ingredient it has become standard.

From Michigan's chefs come many new salads to try—both as an accompaniment to a meal or as the entree. Dressings to be tried with the salads or on salads of your own are here, too.

Asparagus Dill Salad

2 pounds asparagus,
    cut into 1-2" pieces
1½ cups peeled and
    chopped cucumber
1½ cups diced red pepper
1½ cups sliced mushrooms

Dressing:
1½ cups yogurt
½ cup mayonnaise
6 tablespoons minced fresh
    chives
3 tablespoons Dijon mustard
3 tablespoons fresh dill
½ teaspoon salt
½ teaspoon pepper

Steam the asparagus just until bright green. Cool. Then add the other vegetables, toss lightly to mix.

Whisk together the ingredients for the dressing and add to vegetable mixture. Mix gently to thoroughly coat vegetables with dressing. Serve on a bed of fresh lettuce. Garnish with bits of red bell pepper. Yield: 8 cups of salad.

From: **Seva Restaurant**
314 East Liberty Street
Ann Arbor, Michigan

Broccoli Salad

4 cups small broccoli
    flowerets, blanched
1 cup sliced mushrooms
6 slices bacon, cooked,
    crumbled
1 cup raisins, plumped
    in hot water and drained
½ cup chopped red onion
salt and pepper to taste

Dressing:
½ cup good mayonnaise
½ cup sour cream
2 teaspoons fresh lemon juice

Whisk mayonnaise, sour cream and lemon juice together until blended to a smooth consistency. Refrigerate until ready to use.

In a large bowl gently combine the broccoli, mushrooms, bacon, plumped raisins, and onion. Then pour dressing over mixture. Toss salad well, salt and pepper to taste. Yield: 6 servings.

From: **The Bay Pointe Restaurant**
11456 Marsh Road
Shelbyville, Michigan

Bibb Salad
with Raspberry Vinaigrette and Bleu Cheese

Dressing:
½ cup raspberry vinegar
½ cup sugar
1½ cups avocado oil
1 cup heavy cream
1 package frozen rasperries

Salad:
1 head oak leaf lettuce
1 head radicchio
red and yellow apples
mushrooms, thinly sliced
scallions, thinly sliced
crumbled bleu cheese
fresh chopped parsley
bibb lettuce (1 head
   per person)
walnuts
coarse black pepper
fresh raspberries

Defrost frozen raspberries and puree. Place vinegar and sugar in a food processor or blender and dissolve sugar, leave machine running and add oil in thin stream. Add heavy cream and raspberry puree.

Line salad plate with oak leaf and radicchio. On one side make a fan using alternating slices of red and yellow apples. Place bibb in center of plate. Garnish with mushrooms, scallions, and walnuts. Ladle dressing over the top and finally garnish with bleu cheese, parsley, black pepper, and fresh raspberries. Yield: 4 servings.

From: **Stafford's Bay View Inn**
Petosky, Michigan

Marinated Hearts of Palm
and Artichoke Salad

1 can hearts of palm, sliced
1 can artichoke
  hearts, quartered
1 tomato, diced
1 bunch fresh basil chopped
¼ cup olive oil
white wine to taste
1 clove garlic, chopped
juice from 2 lemons
½ tablespoon oregano
¼ tablespoon salt
¼ tablespoon white pepper
Boston lettuce, radicchio,
  and Belgian endive

Mix ingredients together and then toss with hearts of palm, artichoke hearts and tomato and let marinate for two hours. Serve on Boston lettuce, radicchio and Belgian endive. Garnish with carrot flowers if desired. Yield: 4 servings.

From: **Periwinkle's**
          400 West Main Street
          Brighton, Michigan

Proscuitto Mushroom Salad

2 cups mushrooms, thinly
  sliced
1 cup asparagus, cooked
  and cut in ½ " lengths
½ cup canned artichokes
  well drained and diced
¼ cup finely chopped
  prosciutto
⅓ cup rich olive oil
1 tablespoon balsamic
  vinegar
1 large head Bibb
  lettuce, washed
  and dried
1 orange

Slice mushrooms as thinly as possible and mix with the asparagus, artichokes and prosciutto. Just before serving, toss with a dressing made with the olive oil and balsamic vinegar. Serve mixture in a mound on a bed of Bibb lettuce arranged on a plate. Garnish salad with orange slices cut in half. Yield: 6 servings.

From: **Tosi's Restaurant**
          4337 Ridge Road
          Stevensville, Michigan

Spinach Salad
with Breast of Duck
and Raspberry Vinaigrette

Vinaigrette:
*1 tablespoon Dijon
  mustard*
1 egg yolk
1 shallot, minced
*¼ cup raspberry
  vinegar*
¾ cup olive oil
½ teaspoon salt
¼ teaspoon pepper

Salad:
*1 pound spinach, rinsed
  well and dried*
*1 duck breast, sauteed
  medium rare and julienned*
*1 orange, peeled, pith
  removed and sectioned*
*1 head radicchio, torn
  into small pieces*

Mix the Dijon mustard, egg yolk and shallot together. Add the vinegar, stirring steadily. Add the olive oil slowly in a steady stream. Add salt and pepper.

Toss the spinach and raddichio with enough of the vinaigrette to lightly coat. Place on chilled salad plates.

Mix the duck breast with enough vinaigrette to lightly coat and place in the center of each salad. Place four orange segments on each salad and serve. Yield: 4 servings.

From: **Cafe le Chat**
          17001 Kercheval
          Grosse Pointe, Michigan

Tuscan Salad
Creamy Parmesan Dressing

Dressing:
1 cup salad oil
¼ cup red wine vinegar
juice from 1/6 lemon
½ teaspoon salt
½ teaspoon pepper
½ teaspoon garlic powder
½ teaspoon Dijon mustard
1 egg yolk
2 teaspoons sugar
¼ cup freshly grated
   Parmesan cheese

Salad:
1 large head romaine lettuce
2 cups torn iceberg lettuce
¾ cup cooked navy beans
½ cup green beans,
   blanched, cut in half
1 medium tomato, diced
6 large mushrooms,
   sliced
½ red bell pepper,
   diced
¼ cup crumbled bleu cheese
2 green onions, finely
   diced
½ cup freshly grated Parmesan
   cheese, for garnish

Combine the oil, vinegar, lemon juice, salt, pepper, garlic powder, and mustard in a blender and blend well for 10-15 seconds.

Beat together the egg yolk, sugar, and cheese, blending well. Slowly add to mixture in blender while blender is running.

Or combine the egg yolk, sugar, and cheese in a food processor and add the vinaigrette mixture in a slow stream while the machine is running. Yield: Approximately 2 cups of dressing.

Combine all ingredients, except freshly grated Parmesan cheese, in a large bowl and toss with ¾ cup of the Creamy Parmesan Dressing. Garnish with the freshly grated cheese.

From: **The Bay Cafe
at Lumberton**
1050 West Western Avenue
Muskegon, Michigan

Wild Leeks and Watercress Vinaigrette

Vinaigrette:
*4 tablespoons tarragon
 vinegar*
2 teaspoons sweet paprika
*1 teaspoon horseradish-
 style mustard*
1 teaspoon salt
*½ teaspoon cayenne
 pepper*
1 cup mild olive oil
2 teaspoons sugar

Salad:
*½ pound wild leek bulbs,
 white only, cleaned and
 trimmed**
*3 cups wild watercress,
 cleaned and dried*

**Note—Small domestic leeks,
split nearly to the root, cleaned
and parboiled, may be substituted for the wild leeks. Wild leeks,
however, are abundant in most
parts of Michigan.*

Combine all ingredients but oil and sugar in blender jar. Blend till combined, then gradually add the oil till desired thickness and taste is reached (at least ¾ cup oil). Adjust flavor with sugar and more salt and pepper, if desired.

Parboil the leeks in lightly salted water till just tender when pierced with the point of a sharp knife. Immediately drain and rinse with cold water. While still warm, toss with the vinaigrette and marinate for at least 8 hours. The leeks will keep indefinitely if chilled, but serve them at room temperature.

Wild watercress is more variegated in color and more "peppery" in taste than the domesticated. The domestic may be substituted in this recipe. Clean thoroughly and dry.

When ready to serve, pour some of the vinaigrette off the marinating leeks and toss with the sprigs of watercress. Drain off all excess dressing and arrange leeks around the outside of salad plates. Divide the watercress into the center of the plates and sprinkle with freshly cracked pepper.

From: **Tapawingo**
                         9502 Lake Street
                         Ellsworth, Michigan

Wild Rice and Lobster Salad

4 cups cooked wild rice
2 cups lobster meat,
　cut in cubes
2 medium avocados
2 cups chopped tomato,
　peeled and seeded
½ cup chopped red onion
1 tablespoon lemon juice

Vinaigrette:
1 tablespoon Dijon mustard
2½ tablespoons red wine
　vinegar
½ cup olive oil
½ teaspoon garlic
2 tablespoons chopped
　parsley
salt and freshly ground
　pepper to taste

Cook the wild rice according to directions.

Steam lobster in a mixture of water, white wine, parsley sprigs, bay leaf and a few peppercorns. Strain this liquid and freeze for later use in another recipe. Cool lobster until you can handle, cut in cubes and chill.

Peel the avocados and dice into medium cubes. Sprinkle with the lemon juice. Peel and seed the tomatoes and cut into medium dice. (The easiest way to peel tomatoes is to plunge very briefly into boiling water—this loosens the skin very effectively.)

Toss all the above ingredients with the vinaigrette dressing and serve at room temperature. Yield: 4 servings

For vinaigrette dressing, blend all ingredients together until smooth.

From: **Grande Mere Inn**
5800 Red Arrow Highway
Stevensville, Michigan

Basil Salad Dressing

½ cup olive oil
½ cup vegetable oil
½ cup wine or cider
vinegar
⅓ cup minced onions
1 teaspoon minced garlic
½ teaspoon black
pepper
½-1 teaspoon salt, to
taste
2 teaspoons basil, or 2
tablespoons if using fresh
⅓ cup lime juice
½ teaspoon ground ginger
2 tablespoons sugar

Blend all ingredients in blender until well combined.

From: **Traveler's Club
and Tuba Museum**
2138 Hamilton Street
Okemos, Michigan

Creamy Dijon Dressing

1 egg
1 tablespoon white
wine vinegar
1 tablespoon Dijon mustard
⅔ cup corn oil
1 tablespoon lemon juice
3 tablespoons orange juice
1 clove garlic, mashed
½ teaspoon salt
¼ teaspoon black pepper
3 drops Tabasco

Blend the first three ingredients together in a blender. Slowly add in the oil in a thin stream. Add the juices, then the remaining ingredients while continuing to blend.

This dressing is best served on a bed of mixed greens topped with red onion slices, mandarin orange segments and walnuts.

From: **The Victorian Inn**
1229 Seventh Street
Port Huron, Michigan

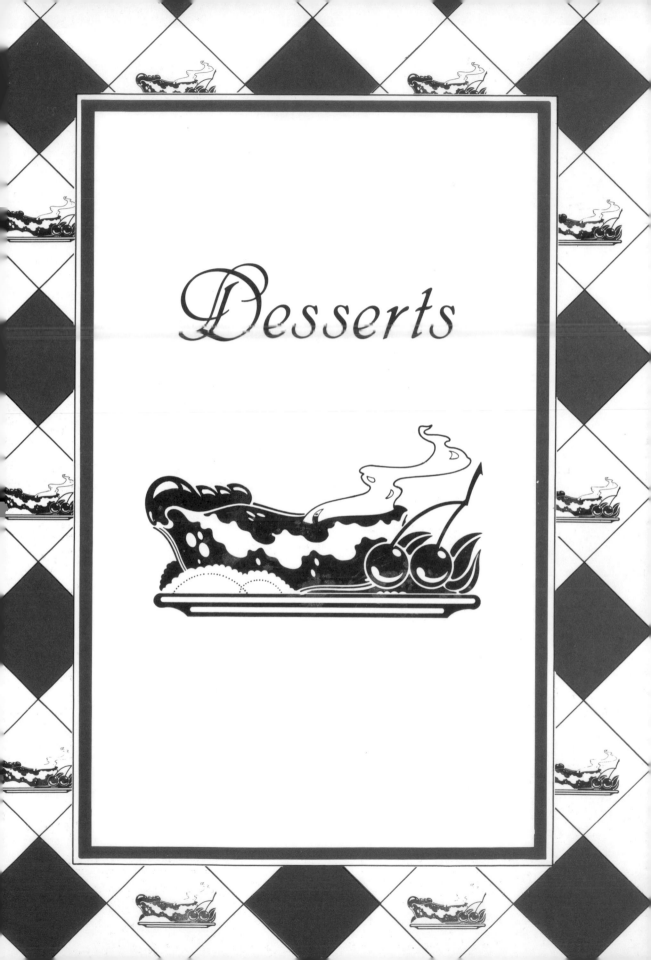

Desserts

Desserts

Dessert is something made to complement the meal; the advantage to restaurant dessert eating is that the choice is so wide. At home we usually make one dessert for a meal, if we make it at all.

Chefs expend a great deal of their creativity on dessert, whether because it's a course that has a faint air of wickedness about it, or whether the ingredients generally used offer such a wide scope in which to work. Whatever the reasons, dessert should be wonderful, a treat, whether it's a simple apple pie or an elaborate confection made for that particular occasion.

Michigan's chefs have responded to the chance to show off what they can do with dessert. There should be something for every palate in this chapter-whether you like apples or strawberries, dark chocolate, ice cream, or old fashioned pudding, or all of them. There are recipes for the beginning cook as well as the more experienced. Read, cook, enjoy!

Apple Walnut Cake
with Rum Sauce

1½ cups vegetable oil
3 eggs
2 cups sugar
2 cups flour
⅛ teaspoon ground cloves
1¼ teaspoons cinnamon
¼ teaspoon ground mace
1 teaspoon baking soda
1¼ teaspoon salt
1 cup whole wheat flour
1¼ cup chopped walnuts
3 cups chopped apples,
　　peeled and cored
3 tablespoons brandy

Rum sauce:
¼ pound butter
¾ cup brown sugar
⅓ cup white sugar
¼ cup orange juice
¼ cup heavy cream
¼ cup light rum

Preheat oven to 325 degrees. Beat vegetable oil and eggs until thick and creamy. Sift together sugar, flour, cloves, cinnamon, mace, baking soda, salt and whole wheat flour. Add gradually to egg and oil mixture, mixing well. Add chopped walnuts, chopped apples, and brandy. Stir until well mixed. Pour into a buttered 9″ springform pan.

Bake for one hour and 15 minutes. Remove from oven and allow cake to rest for 10-15 minutes. Then remove from springform pan. Cut cake and serve warm with rum sauce.

Melt butter in a saucepan. Add both sugars and simmer until sugar dissolves. Add the orange juice, cream, and rum. Cook until slightly thickened and creamy.

From: **Grande Mere Inn**
5800 Red Arrow Highway
Stevensville, Michigan

MacKinnon's Drambuie Cake

½ pound butter
2½ cups sugar
4 eggs
1 teaspoon almond extract
1½ ounces Drambuie or
   Irish whiskey
2½ cups flour
3 tablespoons baking powder
1 teaspoon salt

Preheat the oven to 325 degrees. Put the butter and sugar in the bowl of an electric mixer and mix at medium speed until well blended. Add the eggs, one at a time, beating after each addition. Add the almond extract. Sift the dry ingredients together and add gradually to the wet mixture, beating as you add.

Scrape the batter into a buttered and floured bundt pan or pudding mold. Put in the oven for 1 hour. Test for doneness with a toothpick inserted in the center of the cake.

Remove the cake from the oven, allow to rest for a few minutes. Then turn out onto serving plate. Pour the Drambuie over the cake. Pour on the chocolate mint sauce and serve.

Chocolate mint sauce:
½ pound semisweet
   chocolate
¼ cup heavy cream
Mint liqueur to taste

Melt the chocolate over low heat, beat in the cream, reduce to desired thickness and add the mint liqueur to taste. Pour over cake and serve.

From: **MacKinnon's
of Northville**
126-130 Main Street
Northville, Michigan

Fruit Cocktail Cake

1½ cups sugar
2 cups flour
1 teaspoon baking soda
½ teaspoon salt
1 can (16 ounces) fruit cocktail
2 eggs, slightly beaten
½ cup chopped nuts
½ cup brown sugar

Sauce for cake:
1 stick margarine
1 teaspoon vanilla extract
½ cup evaporated milk
¾ cup sugar
1 cup coconut

Preheat oven to 350 degrees. Sift together the dry ingredients. Add eggs and fruit cocktail to dry ingredients and blend well. Pour into a greased and floured 9″ x 13″ pan. Sprinkle nuts and brown sugar over the top.

Bake in oven for 40 minutes. Remove from oven and allow to cool slightly. Pour hot sauce over the cake.

In medium saucepan add all the ingredients except the coconut. Bring to a boil and cook for 2 minutes, stirring constantly. Remove from the stove and add the coconut. Pour over the cake and serve.

From: **Seney Golden Grill**
Seney, Michigan

Gâteau Nancy
(Light Chocolate Torte)

13 ounces extra bittersweet
    chocolate—any good Swiss
    brand such as Lindt or Tobler's
    will do
½ pound unsalted butter

Timing and blending are essential in this recipe.

In a double boiler, over low heat, melt the chocolate with the butter.

10 eggs, separated
⅛ teaspoon freshly grated
    nutmeg
4 tablespoons sugar
¼ teaspoon cream of tartar
¼ cup finely chopped almonds
1 tablespoon flour
1½ ounces cognac
few drops of vanilla extract
½ cup chopped walnuts

Glaze:
¾ cup brown sugar
½ cup butter
1½ ounces dark rum
1½ ounces brandy
2-3 tablespoons heavy cream
½ cup whole filberts
½ cup chopped walnuts
½ cup chopped almonds
1 large extra bittersweet
    chocolate bar

Using two bowls of the electric mixer, separate the eggs. You may add 2 extra whites to the whites at this point if you wish, to further lighten the torte.

Whip the yolks with the nutmeg until very stiff. Add the chopped almonds to the chocolate mixture, then add the flour, cognac and vanilla.

Add sugar to whipped yolks. Add cream of tartar to egg whites and begin to whip them. Grease either a bundt pan or a 9" springform pan and sprinkle walnuts on the bottom.

Fold your yolk mixture into the chocolate mixture, making sure you work very quickly. Do not overmix. A marble mixture is more desirable than overmixing, if you want a fabulous texture. Immediately add and fold in quickly your egg whites that are smooth, but not dry.

Bake for 22-23 minutes. Let stand in pan before turning out onto serving plate. To serve, prepare glaze that follows and pour over torte.

Cook brown sugar and butter over moderate heat until it carmelizes. Pour in rum, brandy and nuts. Add cream and break in chocolate bar. Heat until chocolate melts. Pour over cooled torte. Yield: 8-10 servings.

From: **Restaurant Duglass**
29269 Southfield
Southfield, Michigan

Frozen Lemon Meringue Torte

4 egg whites
1 cup sugar
½ teaspoon cream of tartar
2 cups heavy cream
1 cup lemon curd
1 teaspoon vanilla extract

Lemon curd:

6 egg yolks
1 cup sugar
½ cup freshly squeezed
   lemon juice
½ cup unsalted butter
1 tablespoon grated
   lemon rind

Preheat oven to 275 degrees. Beat the egg whites until frothy. Add the cream of tartar and beat until soft peaks form. Add sugar 1 tablespoon at a time and continue beating until very stiff peaks form. Add vanilla extract.

Cover a baking sheet with parchment paper. Using an 8" plate, draw two circles on the paper. Divide and spread meringue over each circle shaping into flat shells.

Bake for 45 minutes without opening the oven door. Turn oven off and do not remove meringues for another 45 minutes. Remove and cool.

To make the lemon curd put the egg yolks, sugar and lemon juice in a heavy sauce pan. Cook over low heat stirring constantly until mixture thickens, about 10-12 minutes. Remove from heat, beat in butter 1 tablespoon at a time until fully incorporated. Add rind, cool completely.

To assemble the torte, beat the cream until very stiff, fold in the lemon curd. Spread 1 meringue layer with ½ the lemon cream. Add the second meringue and cover top with remaining cream mixture. Freeze at least six hours. Yield: 10 servings.

From: **The Victorian Inn**
1229 Seventh Street
Port Huron, Michigan

Strawberry Chocolate Shortcake

1 quart ripe strawberries
1 cup heavy cream, whipped

Chocolate Genoise:
6 eggs, room temperature
¾ cup sugar
½ teaspoon vanilla
   extract
1 cup unbleached flour
2 tablespoons cocoa
6 tablespoons unsalted
   butter
4 ounces bittersweet
   chocolate, melted

Chocolate mousse:
11 ounces bittersweet chocolate
6 ounces unsalted butter,
   room temperature
5 egg yolks
8 egg whites (1 cup)
4 tablespoons sugar

Chocolate sauce:
9 ounces bittersweet chocolate
1 cup milk
2 tablespoons heavy cream
¼ cup sugar
3 tablespoons unsalted butter

Preheat oven to 350 degrees. Butter and flour one 11" x 16" jelly roll pan. Place the eggs, sugar and vanilla in the bowl of an electric mixer. Mix well to combine the ingredients and beat at high speed for 10 minutes. The mixture should be pale yellow and triple in volume.

Melt the butter and chocolate over low heat, and cool. Sift together the flour and the cocoa. Gardually fold the flour cocoa mixture into the beaten eggs, then gently fold in the butter chocolate mixture. Fill the prepared pan and bake for 20-25 minutes. Remove from oven and after 5 minutes turn upside down on cooling rack.

Melt the chocolate in a double boiler. Remove from heat and add the butter, stirring it in with a wooden spoon. Allow the mixture to cool, and stir in the egg yolks, one by one.

Beat the egg whites until stiff, halfway through adding in the sugar, a tablespoon at a time. Fold the chocolate mixture into the egg whites with a spatula, making sure the mixture is blended.

Melt the chocolate in a double boiler. In another pan bring the milk to boil, add the cream and bring back to a boil. Remove from the heat, stir in the sugar, the melted chocolate, and the butter. Return to the heat and boil sauce for a few seconds, then pour into a container and allow to cool.

To assemble, use a cookie cutter to cut 3" disks of the chocolate genoise. Cover 8 of the disks with whole and sliced strawberries, then pipe each with approximately ½ cup

chocolate mousse. Cover with another disk of genoise, and top with a dollop of whipped cream. Spoon over 3-4 tablespoons of the chocolate sauce, garnish with fresh, whole strawberries. Yield: 8 servings.

From: **Tapawingo**
9502 Lake Street
Ellsworth, Michigan

MacIntosh Ice Cream

2 cups heavy cream
4 egg yolks
½ cup sugar
1 teaspoon vanilla extract
1 MacIntosh apple, peeled
2 tablespoons butter
2 tablespoons brown sugar
8 ounces apple cider

Place one cup of heavy cream in the top of a double boiler over medium heat. Leave uncovered until a skin forms on top of the cream.

Beat the egg yolks until pale and thick, add sugar gradually and beat for 2-3 minutes. Gradually add half the scalded cream to egg mix, whip together. Add the remaining scalded cream to mix and whip together. Place over a double boiler and cook, stirring constantly, with a rubber spatula until the cream reaches a soft custard consistency.

Remove from heat, stirring constantly, until cool. Add vanilla. Chill for two hours.

Reduce apple cider over low flame to two ounces. Saute apple with butter and brown sugar until soft. Strain and chill. Pour the cream, the custard, reduced apple cider and apple into ice cream freezer and churn until frozen.

From: **Darby's Restaurant**
45199 Cass Avenue
Utica, Michigan

Melon Granite (Ice)

4 pounds melon pulp,
  cantaloupe, honeydew, etc.
2 cups fresh lemon juice
12-16 ounces honey, depending
  on sweetness of melons
10 ounces Cointreau

Peel and seed melons, weigh cleaned pulp. Purée in food processor or blender until no lumps are visible. Add all other ingredients to taste.

Place a small amount of ice mixture in the freezer to test consistency. When completely frozen, if too soft, add more fruit pulp. If too hard, add either Cointreau or honey (or both) and test again.

To complete, either freeze in ice cream machine or pour into a stainless pan and freeze in freezer. When frozen mix into uniform consistency and transfer into a container.

From: **The Golden Mushroom**
18100 West Ten Mile Road
Southfield, Michigan

Pouring Custard

1½ cups milk
⅓ cup sugar
3 egg yolks
½ teaspoon vanilla
  extract

Place all ingredients in small pan and whisk well with a wire whisk. Place over medium heat and cook, stirring constantly, until the mixture coats the back of a metal spoon. Remove from heat. Pour into a suitable container and refrigerate, to be used as needed as a dessert topping.

From: **The Swedish Pantry**
916 Ludington Street
Escanaba, Michigan

Light and Dark Chocolate Pie

Prepare a 9" graham cracker crust and bake it slightly.

2 ounces bitter chocolate
2 ounces butter
1½ cups powdered sugar
2 eggs

3 ounces white chocolate
¾ cup powdered sugar
1 ounce butter
1 egg

1¼ cups heavy cream
½ cup powdered sugar
1 tablespoon cocoa

1¼ cups heavy cream
powdered sugar to taste
½ teaspoon vanilla extract

Melt the chocolate and put in a mixing bowl. Add the butter and sugar and whip at high speed for 3 minutes. Add the eggs, one at a time, at 3 minute intervals. Put the mixture in the pie crust.

Melt the chocolate. Put in mixing bowl. Add butter and sugar and whip for 2 minutes. Add 1 egg and whip for 2 minutes more. Pour into the crust over the previous mixture.

Whip the first three ingredients until stiff peaks form. Put the mixture in a pastry bag, lengthwise. Whip the next three, again until stiff peaks form. Again, put in the pastry bag lengthwise. Pipe the whipped creams through the bag into a decorative design on top of the pie. Chill and serve cold. Yield: 1 9" pie.

From: **The Clarkston Cafe**
18 South Main Street
Clarkston, Michigan

Shaker Lemon Pie

2 lemons
2 cups sugar
4 eggs
pastry for 2 crust
    9" pie

Slice the lemons paper thin and mix well with the sugar. Let stand for at least 2 hours. (This combination may be prepared ahead and will keep well for up to 2 weeks in the refrigerator, tightly covered.)

Preheat oven to 350 degrees. Beat the eggs together and add to the lemon mixture. Put mixture in pie plate and cover with top crust. Crimp edges of crust to seal, cut vents in top, sprinkle with sugar if desired. Bake for 45 minutes or until golden brown.

From: **The Shaker Good Room**
406 West Savidge
Spring Lake, Michigan

Bread Pudding

8 cups diced
    stale coffeecake
¼ cup sugar, unless coffeecake
    is very sweet
½ cup raisins
5 cups scalded milk
3 tablespoons melted butter
4 eggs, beaten

Preheat oven to 350 degrees. Combine all ingredients and mix well. Pour into a buttered 3-quart glass baking dish. Place this dish in a larger pan. Add 1 quart of hot water to the larger pan. Cover the glass dish tightly and bake for 1 hour and 20 minutes or until the top of the pudding is light and springy to the touch. Cool and serve warm with pouring custard or a rum sauce.

From: **The Swedish Pantry**
916 Ludington Street
Escanaba, Michigan

Date and Nut Pudding

3 cups water
3 tablespoons butter
1½ cups dark brown sugar

1½ cups flour
3 teaspoons baking powder
1½ teaspoons cinnamon
¾ cup chopped dates
¾ cup chopped walnuts
⅓-½ cup half & half*

*enough to make stiff batter

Cook until blended.

Preheat oven to 350 degrees. Mix the ingredients in order and put into cooked syrup by tablespoonfuls. Bake in well greased 9" x 12" pan for about 45 minutes. Serve with whipped cream or ice cream. Yield: 12-14 servings.

From: **The Victorian Villa**
601 North Broadway Street
Union City, Michigan

Steamed Plum Pudding

½ cup currants
½ cup seedless raisins
½ cup golden raisins
½ cup candied cherries
½ cup candied pineapple
½ cup pecans
½ cup tart applesauce
1 teaspoon grated lemon peel
1 teaspoon grated orange peel
⅛ cup fresh orange juice
⅛ cup fresh lemon juice
½ cup brandy

½ pound butter, softened
1½ cups flour
3 eggs
3 teaspoons baking powder
½ cup dark brown sugar
¼ teaspoon ground cloves
¼ teaspoon allspice
¼ teaspoon cinnamon
½ cup milk

Combine all the fruit ingredients and and brandy. Let mixture stand in the refrigerator overnight.

Mix all the remaining ingredients together well. Add the fruit mixture and combine well.

Place the mixture in well buttered pudding mold. Place mold in a kettle of hot water and cover the mold tightly with aluminum foil if it doesn't have a cover. Cover the kettle and steam the pudding for 1½-2 hours. Serve warm garnished with holly sprigs. May be served with a hard sauce made with butter, powdered sugar and brandy. Yield: 10-12 servings.

From: **The Victorian Villa**
601 North
Broadway Street
Union City, Michigan

Capirotada
Mexican Bread Pudding

Syrup:
½ gallon water
4 cinnamon sticks
1 tablespoon anise seed
2 pounds dark brown sugar
3 cloves
1 box raisins

2 loaves stale
 French bread
1 pound Muenster
 cheese, shredded
2 cups vegetable oil

Put all ingredients together in a heavy kettle. Bring to a boil, watch carefully as the syrup will have a tendency to boil over. Simmer over medium heat until the syrup has thickened and is dark and honey-like.

Strain the syrup and set syrup and raisins aside. Discard the seeds, cinnamon sticks. Slice the bread. Heat the oil in a deep pan. Deep fry the bread slices, draining them on paper towels.

Preheat oven to 350 degrees. In a large, buttered casserole dish, layer the bread slices with raisins and the shredded cheese. The top layer should be cheese. Each bread slice should be dipped in the syrup before placing in the casserole. Bake in the oven until the ingredients are heated through and the cheese has melted. If there is syrup left, strain it into a sauceboat and serve with the pudding. Do not pour over during baking as it will result in a soggy pudding.

From: **La Fuente de Elena**
3456 West Vernor
Detroit, Michigan

White Mousse

7 ounces white chocolate
10 ounces heavy cream
4 egg whites
⅓ cup sugar

Melt chocolate. Whip the cream until stiff. Whip the egg whites and sugar until stiff peaks form. Fold chocolate into meringue slowly and carefully. Fold chocolate mixture into the whipped cream. Put into individual glass dessert dishes or a single bowl and chill. Serve garnished with mint sprigs. Yield: 8 servings.

From: **Oakley's
at the Haymarket**
161 East Michigan Avenue
Kalamazoo, Michigan

Sauces &

Seasonings

Sauces and Seasonings

Here are a few sauces and seasonings that you can use at your own invention or that are necessary, as in the Ethiopian recipes.

Berbere
Red Pepper and Spice Paste

1 teaspoon ground ginger
½ teaspoon ground
  cardamom
½ teaspoon ground
  coriander
½ teaspoon fenugreek seeds
¾ teaspoon nutmeg,
  preferably freshly grated
⅛ teaspoon ground cloves
⅛ teaspoon ground
  cinnamon
⅛ teaspoon ground allspice
2 tablespoons finely
  chopped onions
1 tablespoon finely
  chopped garlic
2 tablespoons salt
3 tablespoons dry red wine
2 cups paprika
2 tablespoons ground
  hot red peppers
½ teaspoon freshly
  ground black pepper
1½ cups water
1-2 tablespoons
  vegetable oil

In a heavy 2-3 quart enamel or stainless steel saucepan toast the ginger, cardamom, coriander, fenugreek, nutmeg, cloves, cinnamon and allspice over a low heat for 1-2 minutes, stirring them constantly so they are heated through. Then remove the pan from the heat and let the spices cool for 5-10 minutes.

Combine the toasted spices, onions, garlic, 1 tablespoon of the salt, and the wine in a blender, and blend at high speed until the mixture is a smooth paste. To make the paste with a mortar and pestle, or in a bowl with the back of a spoon, pound the toasted spices, onions, garlic and 1 tablespoon of the salt together until they are pulverized. Add the wine and continue pounding until the mixture is moist paste.

Combine the paprika, red pepper, black pepper, and the remaining tablespoon of salt in the saucepan, and toast them over a low heat for a minute or two, until they are heated through, shaking the pan and stirring the spices constantly. Stir in the water, a ¼ cup at a time, then add the spice and wine mixture. Stirring vigorously, cook over the lowest possible heat for 10-15 minutes.

With a rubber spatula, transfer the berbere to a jar or crock, and pack it in tightly. Let the paste cool to room temperature, then dribble enough oil over the top to make a film at least ¼" thick. Cover with foil or plastic wrap and refrigerate until ready to use. If you replace the film of oil each time you use the berbere, it can be kept safely in the refrigerator for 5-6 months.

From: **The Blue Nile**
Trappers Alley
508 Monroe Street
Detroit, Michigan

Hawaiian Marinade

This marinade is good for fish or chicken.

¼ cup brown sugar
1 bottle Rose's lime juice
1 (32 ounce) can
  pineapple juice
2 ounces whole black
  peppercorns
2 large tomatoes, chopped
1 tablespoon fresh garlic
1 pineapple, cut in chunks
4 bay leaves, crushed
¼ cup olive oil
½ red onion, chopped
1 tablespoon soy sauce
¼ cup sesame oil

Blend all ingredients together. Refrigerate the mixture 5 hours. Re-blend mixture thoroughly before using. This marinade is especially tasty when used with blue marlin fish or chicken breasts. Marinate the fish for 30 minutes, the chicken breasts for 15 minutes.

From:
The Bay Pointe Restaurant
11456 Marsh Road
Shelbyville, Michigan

Lingonberry Sauce for Roast Duck

2 ounces demi-glace
2 ounces sweet vermouth
2 ounces raspberry vinegar
2 ounces heavy cream
2 ounces currant jelly
3 ounces lingonberries
  in heavy syrup

Combine all ingredients together in a saucepan. Heat gently and slowly and reduce to desired thickness.

Bake duck in oven at 250 degrees for 2 hours and 15 minutes. Serve with Lingonberry Sauce.

From:
The Holly Hotel
110 Battle Alley
Holly, Michigan

Niter K'ibe
Spiced Butter

2 pounds unsalted butter,
   cut into small pieces
1 small onion, peeled and
   coarsely chopped
3 tablespoons finely chopped
   garlic
4 teaspoons finely chopped
   fresh ginger root
6 tablespoons fresh basil
4 teaspoons fresh rue seed
¼ teaspoon fenugreek seeds,
   pounded
1 cardamom pod, slightly
   crushed with the flat of
   knife, or pinch of cardamom
   seeds
1 1"-cinnamon stick
⅛ teaspoon nutmeg,
   preferably freshly grated
1½ teaspoons turmeric

In a heavy 4-5 quart saucepan, heat the butter over a moderate heat, stirring it with a spoon to melt slowly without browning. Increase the heat and bring the butter slowly to a boil. When the surface is completely covered with white foam, stir in the onion, garlic, ginger, fresh basil, and rue seed. When it is simmering, add the fenugreek, cardamom, cinnamon, clove and nutmeg. Reduce the heat as low as possible. Add turmeric and simmer uncovered, and undisturbed for 45 minutes, or until the milk solids on the bottom of the pan are a golden brown and the butter on the top is clear.

Slowly pour the clear liquid spiced butter into a bowl, straining it through a fine sieve lined with a linen towel or four layers of dampened cheesecloth. If there are any solids left in the butter, strain it again to prevent it from becoming rancid later.

Pour the butter into a jar, cover tightly and store in the refrigerator or at room temperature until ready to use. Butter will solidify when chilled. It can be kept safely, even at room temperature, for 2-3 months.

From: **The Blue Nile**
Trappers Alley
508 Monroe Street
Detroit, Michigan

Spicy Cheese Sauce for Hot Vegetables

This is excellent served over broccoli, cauliflower, beans or potatoes.

½ cup olive oil
4 tablespoons chopped green chilies
1¾ cups sharp cheddar cheese
1½ pounds cream cheese, softened
½ pound Muenster cheese
2 cups water
½ cup cornstarch
2 cups milk
2 teaspoons white pepper

Heat olive oil and saute chilies for 1-2 minutes. Add cheeses and stir as they begin to melt. Dissolve the cornstarch in ½ cup of the water. Slowly add the remaining water to this mixture, then stir into the melted cheeses. Add milk and white pepper. Stir constantly while bringing to a simmer over low heat. Blend thoroughly.

From: **Traveler's Club
and Tuba Museum**
2138 Hamilton Street
Okemos, Michigan

Inns & Restaurants

The numbers inside the parentheses (   ) after the name of the restaurant indicate the pages on which recipes from that restaurant appear. Unless otherwise specified, reservations are not necessary.

ANN ARBOR

Argiero's Restaurant
300 Detroit Street
Ann Arbor
313/665-0440
Reservations appreciated
No credit cards
(6, 96)

The Moveable Feast
326 West Liberty
Ann Arbor
313/663-3278
Reservations appreciated
Luncheon and dinner served
No credit cards
Also at: 407 North 5th Avenue
Takeout from Tote Cuisine
(36, 87, 98)

Seva Restaurant
314 East Liberty
Ann Arbor
313/662-2019
Reservations encouraged
Credit Cards: V, MC
(16, 24, 46, 52, 101)

A Slice of Heaven
116 South Main
Ann Arbor
313/663-8830
No credit cards
(25, 27, 37)

DETROIT and SUBURBS

Antonio's Restaurant
20311 Mack Avenue
Grosse Pointe Woods
313/884-0253
Reservations suggested
Credit Cards: V, MC
(11, 15, 73)

The Blue Nile
Trapper's Alley
508 Monroe Street
Detroit
313/964-6699
Reservations recommended
Credit Cards: V, MC, AE
(19, 60, 72, 97, 127, 129)

Cafe le Chat
17001 Kercheval
Grosse Pointe
313/884-9077
Reservations recommended
Credit Cards: V, MC
(33, 66, 104)

Chez Raphael
27000 Sheraton Drive
Novi
313/348-5555
Reservations necessary
Credit Cards: V, MC, AE, CB, DC
(7, 74)

The Clarkston Cafe
18 South Main Street
Clarkston
313/625-5660
Reservations recommended for dinner
Credit Cards: V, MC, AE
(75, 119)

Darby's
45199 Cass Avenue
Utica
313/731-4440
Reservations necessary
Credit Cards: V, MC, AE, DC
(55, 68, 94, 117)

La Fuente de Elena
3456 West Vernor
Detroit
313/842-8277
No credit cards
Also: **Elena's Restaurant**
317 Michigan Avenue
Detroit
313/965-6688
(63, 123)

Garden Cafe
Detroit Gallery of Contemporary Crafts
301 Fisher Building
Detroit
313/873-7888
No credit cards
(54)

The Golden Mushroom
18100 West 10 Mile Road
Southfield
313/559-4230
Reservations necessary
Credit Cards: V, MC, AE, CB, DC
(52, 69, 98, 118)

Holly Hotel
110 Battle Alley
Holly
313/634-5208
Reservations recommended
Credit Cards: V, MC, AE, CB, DC
(48, 128)

MacKinnon's
126-130 East Main Street
Northville
313/348-1991
Reservations encouraged
Credit Cards: V, MC, AE
(34, 112)

The Money Tree
333 West Fort and Washington Boulevard
Detroit
313/961-2445
Reservations necessary
Credit Cards: V, MC, AE, CB, DC
(36, 76, 90)

Monte Bianco Restaurant
962 Dix Street
Lincoln Park
313/388-7092
Reservations appreciated
Credit Cards: V, MC, AE, CB, DC
(6)

Periwinkle's
400 West Main
Brighton
313/229-4115
Reservations recommended
Credit Cards: V, MC, DC
(47, 56, 61, 103)

Polish Village Cafe
2990 Yeamans, east of Jos Campau
Hamtramck
313/873-2502
No credit cards
(50, 95)

Restaurant Duglass
29269 Southfield
Southfield
313/424-9244
Reservations necessary
Credit Cards: V, MC, AE, DC
(45, 50, 80, 113)

Richard and Reiss
273 Pierce Street
Birmingham
313/645-9122
Breakfast and Luncheon cafeteria style
Reservations preferred for dinner
No credit cards
(65)

Ristorante di Maria
2080 Walnut Lake Road
West Bloomfield
313/851-2500
Reservations recommended: open dinner only
Credit Cards: V, MC
(68, 79, 81)

The Whitney
4421 Woodward Avenue
Detroit
313/832-5700
Reservations necessary for dinner
Credit Cards: V, MC
(32)

KALAMAZOO

The Ample Pantry
5629 Stadium Drive
Kalamazoo
616/375-8300
Luncheon 11:30-1:30 Mon.-Sat.
No credit cards
(5, 35, 95)

Oakley's at the Haymarket
161 East Michigan Avenue
Kalamazoo
616/349-6436
Reservations recommended
Credit Cards: V, MC, AE
(44, 67, 124)

Sarkozy's Bakery & Cafe
335 North Burdick Street
Kalamazoo
616/342-1952
No credit cards
(13, 22, 26)

South Street Culinary Shoppe
116 West South Street
Kalamazoo
616/385-0500
No credit cards
(38, 83)

MICHIGAN INNS and RESTAURANTS

Arie's Cafe
127 East Bridge Street
Plainwell
616/685-9495
Take out available
No credit cards
(70, 89)

The Bay Cafe at Lumbertown
1050 West Western Avenue
Muskegon
616/728-7272
Reservations appreciated
Credit Cards: V, MC, AE
(4, 88, 105)

The Bay Pointe Restaurant
11456 Marsh Road
Shelbyville
616/672-5202
Reservations recommended
Credit cards: V, MC, AE
(44, 64, 86, 101, 128)

Brandywine Pub and Food
2125 Horton Road
Jackson
517/783-2777
Reservations suggested
Credit Cards: V, MC, AE
(8, 94)

Grande Mere Inn
5800 Red Arrow Highway
Stevensville
616/429-3591
Reservations appreciated,
   necessary on weekends
Credit Cards: V, MC, AE
(31, 84, 107, 111)

The Hearthstone
3550 Glade (Corner House Motel)
Muskegon
616/733-1056
Credit Cards: V, MC, AE
(3, 14, 49)

Justine
5010 Bay City Road
Midland
517/496-3012
Reservations advisable
Credit Cards: V, MC, AE
(10, 39)

Kola's Kitchen
4500 13th Street
Wyandotte
313/283-4700
No credit cards
(62)

Leelanau Country Inn
149 East Harbor Highway
Maple City
616/228-5060
Reservations necessary
Credit Cards: V, MC
(53)

The Rowe Inn
County Road C48
Ellsworth
616/588-7351
Reservations recommended
Credit Cards: V, MC
(40, 43, 59)

Seney Golden Grill
Seney
No credit cards
No reservations
(113)

The Shaker Good Room
406 West Savidge
Spring Lake
616/846-4202
No credit cards
(19, 120)

Stafford's Bay View Inn
P.O. Box 3
Petosky
616/347-2771
Reservations necessary
Credit Cards: V, MC, AE
(71, 96, 102)

The Swedish Pantry
916 Ludington Street
Escanaba
906/766-9606
Credit Cards: V, MC
(9, 23, 46, 118, 120)

Tapawingo
9502 Lake Street
Ellsworth
616/588-7971
Reservations necessary
Credit Cards: V, MC
(21, 55, 106, 116)

Thornapple Village Inn
455 Thornapple Village, SE
Ada
616)676-1233
Reservations recommended
Credit Cards: V, MC, AE
(85)

Tosi's
4337 Ridge Road
Stevensville
616/429-3689
Reservations recommended
Credit Cards: V, MC
(12, 51, 97, 103)

Traveler's Club and Tuba Museum
2138 Hamilton Street
Okemos
517/349-1701
No credit cards
(48, 93, 108, 130)

The Victorian Inn
1229 Seventh Street
Port Huron
(313/984-1437
Reservations necessary
No cards
(82, 108, 115)

The Victorian Villa
601 North Broadway Street
Union City
517/741-7383
Reservations necessary
No credit cards
(28, 121, 122)

Index

Q

R

S

T